Sonora

of map

San Francisco
Stockton
Present
Yosemite National
Park

Pacheco Pass
San Joaquin R.

Big Oak Flat

CALIFORNIA

0   100   200   300
Miles

Horseshoe Bend

Modern road
to Yosemite Park

Present Ex-
chequer Dam

Merced River

Johnsonville (now Bear Valley)

Indian Reservation

Present town of
Merced Falls
Belt's Tent

Washington Mine
Quartzburg

Gaines
Ledge

Dry Creek

Snelling's Ranche

Number Nine

Mt. Ophir

Mariposa

Indian Rancheria
Belt's Ferry & Store

"MT. SAVAGE"

Hornitos

Agua Fria
Mormon Bar

Phillips' Ferry & Store

River

Burns Creek

Greaser Gulch

Bear Creek

Frémont's Mari-
posa Grant,as
first claimed

Howard Bros' Ranche

Present city
of Merced

Mariposa Creek

Frémont's Ranche

Raisz

Chappell

OP 10th

Sam Ward
in the Gold Rush

Samuel Ward

SAM WARD

in the

GOLD

RUSH

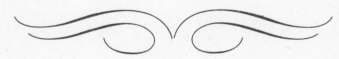

Edited by

Carvel Collins

Stanford University Press
Stanford, California

STANFORD UNIVERSITY PRESS
CALIFORNIANA ADVISORY COMMITTEE

DONALD P. BEAN
HAROLD W. BRADLEY
CHILTON R. BUSH
WILLIAM HAWLEY DAVIS
FRANCIS P. FARQUHAR
GEORGE L. HARDING
JOSEPH HENRY JACKSON
GEORGE D. LYMAN
EDGAR E. ROBINSON
MAXWELL H. SAVELLE
CARL I. WHEAT
OSCAR O. WINTHER

STANFORD UNIVERSITY PRESS, STANFORD, CALIFORNIA
LONDON: GEOFFREY CUMBERLEGE, OXFORD UNIVERSITY PRESS

THE BAKER AND TAYLOR COMPANY, 55 FIFTH AVENUE, NEW YORK 3
HENRY M. SNYDER & COMPANY, 440 FOURTH AVENUE, NEW YORK 16
W. S. HALL & COMPANY, 457 MADISON AVENUE, NEW YORK 22

Copyright 1949 by the Board of Trustees of the Leland Stanford Junior University
Printed and Bound in the United States of America
by Stanford University Press

Preface

TWO YEARS ago while examining the ninth volume (1861) of the New York weekly called *Porter's Spirit of the Times*, I found that it contained a few opening installments of a serial memoir of the California Gold Rush. The possible interest of the memoir to present-day readers made it seem suitable for reprinting in our time—especially so because in its original form it was almost inaccessible, only two complete copies of that ninth volume being known to exist. But too few installments were available, and to search for more seemed futile because reference guides stated that *Porter's Spirit* stopped publication at the conclusion of the ninth volume. Recently, however, a complete copy of a hitherto unknown tenth volume of the periodical came by luck into my possession; and when it was found to contain several more installments, reprinting the greatly enlarged memoir as a book became possible.

One problem remained—discovering the identity of the author, who had hidden behind a pseudonym, signing himself "Midas, Jr." The search eventually led to a manuscript of legal testimony in the National Archives which gave simultaneously the first hint and the final proof that "Midas, Jr." was Samuel Ward—brother of Julia Ward Howe, companion of Longfellow, friend of Thackeray, epicure, poet of sorts, and "King of the Lobby."

In the interest of readability the text has been altered as follows: Digressions of little interest as well as especially wordy passages have been omitted, with all omissions indicated by ellipses except at the beginning of Numbers One, Three, and Eleven, where ellipses interfered with design. Obvious typographical and spelling errors have been corrected without indication. Where irrationality of punctuation made sentences difficult, the punctuation has been changed.

Further in the interest of readability, no formal references to sources of information are given. But a bibliographical note at the back of the book gives general references to sources, and an interleaved copy of the book containing detailed references will be deposited at the Stanford University Library.

CARVEL COLLINS

HARVARD UNIVERSITY
September 1948

Contents

List of Illustrations

ix

SAM WARD

in the

GOLD
RUSH

Introduction

ON JUNE 4, 1849, the new side-wheeler *Panama* entered San Francisco Bay on her first voyage, one hundred eight days out of New York and burning her planking to keep up steam. Among the passengers crowded on deck as she worked toward her mooring were three relatives who had taken the trip together round the Horn, bringing goods with which they hoped to become San Francisco merchants. Hall McAllister, just twenty-three, was soon to be the leading lawyer of California. His younger brother, Ward McAllister, was to leave the West Coast after a few years and become a social arbiter of New York–Newport society, creating "The Four Hundred" by his pruning of a guest list. With them was their cousin, Sam Ward, aged thirty-five, then at one of the lowest points of his life's astonishingly fluctuating fortune. In a letter written aboard the *Panama* he had told his sister, "I am too old to hope and not old enough to be indifferent . . . . I cannot see any bright prospect ahead"; but as he stared across the Bay at the capital of the Gold Rush he may have consoled himself with the thought that however empty the future seemed he had considerable to remember from the past.

The eldest son of a wealthy banker of New York, he had spent his childhood in that city, in Newport, and on the Long Island farm of his grandfather. Up to the age of nine he was trained for the most part by private tutors; he then went to Round Hill School at Northampton, which was directed by George Bancroft and Joseph Cogswell,

3

both of whom had been in the early wave of Americans to be educated in Germany.

At Round Hill, as later, he showed proficiency in learning languages. He also showed, to George Bancroft at least, the fault of character which was to cause many of his future difficulties. Bancroft wrote to the senior Samuel Ward that Sam was intelligent and talented and quick but that he had never learned discipline. On leaving the school, where he had made a lifelong friend of Cogswell, Sam entered Columbia University and was graduated in three years, at the age of seventeen.

During the next year he studied mathematics, worked on a new edition of Young's *Algebra*, and published the *Mathematical Diary*. He also wrote reviews. During that year he was elected secretary of the New York Historical Society and, despite his eighteen years, served on the board of examiners at West Point and was offered, according to his own account, an assistant professorship there.

His father had always maintained toward him an attitude of severity, which grew in part from grief at the early death of Sam's mother and in part from great hope for the future of this eldest son. But the father was capable of surprising indulgence, for when the eighteen-year-old boy who had always been so closely supervised asked to spend a year abroad alone, his father consented.

He invaded Europe with a large letter of credit and an imposing group of letters of introduction, some of them written by Albert Gallatin. They included one to the Perpetual Secretary of the Académie des Sciences, which was of great use to Sam, and another to the president of a missionary society, which Sam made no use of whatever. At the end of 1832 he was at Paris, settled in the Latin Quarter, and had sent to his father the first of several letters explaining why expenses were heavier than seemed possible. That he quickly began to associate with distinguished Parisians is surprising to us, but as Maud Howe Elliott points out in *Uncle Sam Ward and His Circle*, young Americans in Paris with such funds and such introductions were rare, and, in addition, Sam then and always justified his friend Charles Sumner's remark that he was "the most delightful company in the world."

So, with his money, his connections, and his charm, he found himself in the artistic and intellectual circles of the Paris of the eighteen-thirties. The critic and author Jules Janin, who is said to have had Sam in mind when he wrote *The American in Paris*, became his close friend and helped him write reviews for French periodicals. Liszt played at small Sunday breakfasts which Sam attended. Paganini permitted Sam to hear him practice. At the soiree where Ole Bull made his debut as a professional violinist, Sam made his debut as an amateur singer. He studied languages. He studied mathematics. He was elected to membership in the Société de Géographie, and he worked on a biography of Locke. Despite this scattering of his energies, he was eager to become a scholar and was undoubtedly sincere when he told his father that he had bought the large and expensive mathematical library of Legendre because he *"needed the best books."*

His letters home were full of these associations and occupations. But he also was taking part in the life of the students of the Sorbonne and the Collège de France, some of which he recorded in an intimate journal. The one year in Europe that had been planned he was able to stretch into four, in part by practicing on his father the same minor deceptions that the young Longfellow, seven years older than Sam and later to become one of his closest friends, had practiced a few years earlier. Useful devices which they both discovered included well-timed reports of hard study and equally well-timed removals to new addresses when they expected letters ordering them home.

5

Sam found that even the elastic purse supplied him by his father could not stretch far enough to pay without interruption for his life in Paris; so to economize he visited Germany. There he found the life of Heidelberg interesting, in part because an eccentric baron took him in as a paying guest and became his friend. There he learned the songs that were to enrapture his relatives on future evenings around the piano in New York and Newport. There he continued to develop the taste that he had acquired in Paris for good foods and wines, a taste which was to be one of his vocational assets as "King of the Lobby" a quarter-century later. There in 1834 he wrote a thesis which not only won a Ph.D. from Tübingen but also further concessions from his father, who permitted him to continue traveling about in his private carriage between Paris, Berlin, and Heidelberg.

He became the unpaid secretary of the American Legation in Berlin. He sat for his portrait by Von Vogelstein. He spent some time at Dresden with George Ticknor and his family. He called on Karl Gauss in 1835 and astonished the scientist by remembering an equation from one of Gauss's books which would solve the astronomy problem they were discussing. And in Heidelberg in 1836, at a small reception for Mrs. William Cullen Bryant, he met Longfellow for the first time and began the close friendship that was to last until Longfellow's death in 1882.

After a visit with Longfellow to the Baron at Heidelberg, and a visit to the home in Luxemburg of Charles Mersch, a student friend whom he was in part supporting, Sam found that this relatively carefree European period must end. He had stayed four years and spent $16,000, and could not ignore his father's demand that he come home, at once and without passing through Paris *unless absolutely necessary.*" He left Mersch and the Baron and

6

the scenes that were later to furnish some of his most romantic memories, but it was *"absolutely necessary"* to pass through Paris. And when he arrived there it seemed equally necessary to remain for a while.

Finally, in July 1836, he started home. On the way he stopped in England and, at the suggestion of a member of the financial house of Baring Brothers, took a tour to study Britain's industries. In London, through Joseph Bonaparte, the ex-king of Spain, he first came to know Adolphe Mailliard, who later was to marry one of his sisters and to join him in San Francisco during the Gold Rush. Before he left England Sam called on Murray, who he hoped would one day be his publisher.

Arriving in New York in October 1836, he at once became an apprentice in the family's banking house, against his inclination and his training. His early European years were over, but their effect on him would be plain throughout his life.

In New York he kept regular business hours, but he also kept his dreams of authorship. He wrote Charles Mersch, "I must be rich, and so, for a few years I must work"; but he urged his friend to come from Luxemburg to join the Ward household and begin preliminary labor on the great book they would write together. In 1838, after many persuasive letters, Mersch came.

Much of Sam's life in this period was pleasant despite the uncongeniality of business. He was happily married to Emily Astor, granddaughter of John Jacob Astor. He enjoyed giving lectures before the New York Historical Society and the Mercantile Library Association, and writing reviews and articles. With Mersch he spent comfortable evenings of study in his well-stocked library, and he took pleasure in pulling wires in an effort to get Mersch a professorship at Harvard.

He regularly visited Cambridge, where he belonged

to "The Five of Clubs," a congenial group which included Samuel Gridley Howe, later to marry Sam's sister Julia, the author-to-be of "The Battle Hymn of the Republic." Through these Cambridge associations and because of his articles in the periodicals of the day, Sam was made a member of the Harvard chapter of Phi Beta Kappa.

In New York he spent considerable time with Fitz-Greene Halleck, saw something of the visiting Charles Dickens, and corresponded with Washington Irving, then in Paris, who said that he learned much about home affairs from Sam that he did not learn from any other friend.

One of his satisfying associations in this period was with Longfellow. The two men visited and corresponded frequently, sometimes writing to each other almost daily for weeks at a time. Longfellow's letters to Sam have been called the most indiscreet he ever wrote. Most of the mild indiscretions grew out of his interest in Fanny Elssler, the dancer. That Longfellow thought her virtuous amused Sam, but he implemented the poet's worship by sending him her statue and by showing great willingness to carry on a discussion of her charms by mail. Sam found Longfellow a link to the life which he longed for and hoped to become a part of in the near future, when he could abandon Wall Street. Longfellow found Sam a loyal and entertaining companion who shared his love of European culture, especially German romanticism. And he found Sam, as did others, one to make himself useful to a friend. He placed Longfellow's poems with publishers, bargaining shrewdly about the price. He was a source of literary ideas, giving Longfellow the basic suggestions for "The Skeleton in Armor" and "The Phantom Ship" and persuading him to translate certain foreign works. From time to time, frequently at Longfellow's request and frequently not, he suggested poetic revisions. During the period before Longfellow's financial problems were solved, Sam

loaned him money, a favor Longfellow was to return in
1857 when their positions were reversed. In 1839 Sam
did what he could to arrange that his brother-in-law, the
grandson of John Jacob Astor, should take Longfellow
abroad for five or six years as his guide and tutor. Sam
pointed out to the poet that in the long run it would be
better to keep his Harvard professorship, but Longfellow
was eager for the chance to return to Europe and was disappointed by the Astors' decision that the boy should go
alone. When Longfellow in 1842 did take a trip abroad,
which he felt he needed for his health, Sam loaned
him money and wrote introductions to European friends,
among them Jules Janin, who Longfellow hoped might
introduce him to George Sand. When Longfellow returned to the United States and married Fanny Appleton,
Sam Ward was once again on hand, taking charge of the
wedding's social detail.

During these early years of Sam's amiable association
with literary and scholarly men and ideas there was much
sorrow in his family life. In three years four members of
his family died: in 1839 his father, in 1840 his brother
Henry, and in 1841 his wife, Emily Astor Ward, at the
birth of their second child, a boy, who survived his mother
only a few days. In 1847 death took his younger brother,
Marion, to whom he was closely drawn and without whom
he felt rudderless.

In 1843 Sam married Medora Grymes, whose father
was a prominent resident of New Orleans. She was a great
beauty and according to *Harper's Weekly* was "considered
by New York artists as an incarnation of Aphrodite." But
James Brevoort, in writing to Washington Irving about
the match, expressed the opinion that Sam had probably
made a mistake; unfortunately Brevoort's judgment was
correct, for this second marriage turned out to be unhappy.

The sorrows and difficulties in his family were not

Sam Ward's only troubles during this period. His financial situation, which began to erode shortly after the death of his father, rapidly grew worse, until his funds and position were entirely washed away. His father had held large sections of New York City real estate, but following his death a brother, as administrator, showed little ability in handling these investments. In 1846 Sam quarreled with a partner in his father's banking house and formed a new partnership. In 1847, at the time of the death of his brother Marion, who had proved to be the only good financier in his generation of the family, this new firm failed and Sam was almost penniless.

His daughter by his first marriage had been taken to live with the Astors; now his wife and their two sons went to live with her father in New Orleans, while Sam stayed in New York doing what he could to make a living. After news of the California gold discovery reached the East, he scraped together what money he could find to buy a ticket and a supply of suitable merchandise, paid a gloomy round of visits to his relatives in New York and Boston, and with his two McAllister cousins and his friend Mersch sailed in February 1849 on the *Panama*, bound round the Horn.

His life up to 1849 has been fully described in Maud Howe Elliott's biography and in other studies, but his California years have remained somewhat mysterious because of a lack of documents. Mrs. Elliott says, "Inveterate correspondent as he was, only four letters of this epoch survive. . . . ." And the *New York Herald* reported in an obituary that he had been in the California mines, but "what he did and where he went nobody ever knew." Part of the mystery is cleared by the discovery of the autobiographical account being republished here, which describes his experiences in the Southern Mines during 1851 and 1852. Further information about his California years has come to light in an examination of local historical materials.

When he reached San Francisco he wasted no time in becoming a participant in the city's affairs. On June 11, 1849, he signed with others a broadside inviting his "fellow citizens" to hold a meeting in Portsmouth Square to consider "the necessity of electing Delegates to a Convention to form a Government for Upper California," Congress "having adjourned without doing anything for the neglected people." This, in the first week after he landed.

Rumor says that soon after his arrival in California, he went to the diggings, sold his goods there, and tried mining. But it seems doubtful that he left the city in 1849. In June he signed the broadside already described. In the next month he was one of those who, with such prominent citizens as Sam Brannan and C. V. Gillespie, called a meeting on the Plaza and organized the "Law and Order Party" to arrest and try "The Hounds," a band of cutthroats. At the end of July he was among the forty-one men who signed the preamble to the constitution of the First California Guard.

These documents showing that he was active in the interests of the community are not the only evidence that he was then probably too busy in the city to spend much, if any, time in the mines. That he was equally occupied in San Francisco with his own business affairs is suggested by a few other bits of information. In the summer of 1849 he seems to have become a member of the group that had built and was successfully managing Long Wharf, the first such venture in California. Perhaps through their association as members of the Long Wharf company, he and Rodman M. Price became partners in the firm of Ward & Price and opened a mercantile and auction house, which quickly made Sam rich—according to rumor. Ac-

Long Wharf, at San Francisco, California

cording to his own testimony, he made at least enough profit to own $40,000 worth of San Francisco real estate; and one of his remarks in a letter to Longfellow years afterward suggested that all told he made a quarter of a million. His partner, Price, later to be governor of New Jersey, had come to California as a naval officer in 1846 and had begun as early as 1847 to buy property so avidly that by 1850–51 he owned more San Francisco houses than any other man. Sam joined this sort of speculation, and his name appeared during 1849 in several transfers of deeds, the latest one taking place in December, when he bought a lot on Mission Street for $12,000.

Sociable as ever, Sam did not spend all his energy on public meetings, his partnership with Price, or real estate deals. When a banquet was to be given in a large warehouse where the lighting was inadequate, "the versatile Sam Ward, known in later years as 'Uncle Sam,' came to the rescue," according to the reminiscences of one resident of San Francisco, and when "the night arrived, the guests found the sides of the room lined with marble statues, holding blazing flambeaux of pitch pine, the statues being stevedores, stripped and whitewashed."

Sam had met Jessie Benton Frémont when she made the trip north from the Isthmus on the steamer *Panama*, and they kept up their acquaintance after reaching California. He gave her the copy of *Kavanagh* which Longfellow sent to him at San Francisco as soon as it came off the press, and he took part in the social life that she described in her unpublished memoirs:

. . . . Mr. Frémont bought a ready made chinese-built house which fitted together like a puzzle. . . . . Pleasant men rode over constantly when the day ended, and in frontier fashion ate with us. It could not be called "dining" for that implies so many adjuncts then unattainable, but we had now all the resources of San Francisco, while keen high vitality and the exhilaration

13

of unexpected and great success, added their spur to the many
charming men who had come out in quest of a short cut to fortune, and found it . . . . the Bay and the sand dunes with their
flowering lupines made our framing, while we sat at meat by the
unused bundles of shingles which made our tables . . . . we
certainly were all in great content, and the blending of open air
and camping with every delicate luxury for the table made a pi-
quant combination. And I was a great feature, for any lady was
a rarity, but I was of their people and memories. Mr. Frémont
found Mr. Ward, "Sam Ward" of epicurean fame, a most agreeable man. He had been a fellow passenger on my steamer and I
had had many thoughtful kindnesses from him. Our friends the
Commissioners too, and "fighting Joe Hooker" then a slim young
army officer; and pleasant Dr. Bowie with all the courtesy and
generosity of his Maryland family, and eccentric "Ned" Beale.
While others, less known but men very interesting to me from
their travelled lives in China and India and South America, all
gave animated variety to our shingle-pack table and the prolonged
talks around our camp fire; then from the men's camp would be
summoned the waiting horses and the groups of horsemen would
vanish over the dunes. To me, it was all a most charming episode, that California of 1849.

Sam was to see more of the Frémonts, for when they
sailed on the first day of 1850 aboard the *Oregon* for the
Isthmus crossing, he was among their fellow passengers.
He had given his San Francisco bankers, Godeffroy &
Sillem, the power of attorney over his California affairs
and was off to New York to establish at 54 Wall Street
the main office of Ward & Price, "Bankers and Agents for
California." The success of the first phase of the Gold
Rush was apparent in the bullion shipment aboard the
Oregon that voyage, for according to Bayard Taylor,
another of the passengers, it was "the most important
which had ever left San Francisco," Taylor somewhat
overestimating it as "about two millions of dollars." Sam
Ward had had his share of the general success, and it is

possible that he thought he was returning permanently to New York.

If so, he was to be disappointed, for the financial ventures of Ward & Price, which one source says included speculation in steamship lines, did not prosper during 1850. The firm contracted large debts, including among its creditors Sam's uncle, John Ward, of New York; his uncle, Hall McAllister, Sr.; and, ironically enough, his formerly impoverished European protégé, Charles Mersch, who had become one of the San Franciscans wealthy enough to be listed in that curious volume of 1851, *A "Pile."*

Sam sailed into San Francisco Bay once again on January 4, 1851, and began four years of what he later testified was uninterrupted residence in California. He resumed his real estate operations, but the transactions of 1851 which bear his name indicate shrinking fortunes. He was not alone in his financial troubles during the early part of that year, however, for one California paper said in January, "These are hard times, truly. Every branch of industry and commerce is in an unprecedented depressed state . . . ." Then came the great San Francisco fires of 1851, which wiped out the firm of Ward & Price, according to several not entirely reliable sources. Whether or not the fires were what ruined Sam Ward, it is certain that when Price, who also had been in the East, arrived in San Francisco on July 19, 1851, Sam, according to his own statement, "abandoned to him here, and to Francis Griffin at home . . . . all that I possessed[,] he undertaking to pay the debts of the firm." Price apparently held himself equally at fault with Ward in the failure of their partnership, for they remained friends, had some business associations, and later co-operated in a lawsuit in which Price sought to recover a half-million dollars from his California agents.

But no matter who was responsible, Sam Ward had

lost the second of his three fortunes and again had to cast about to make a living. In one of his few extant letters from California he wrote that from May of 1851 until September "my time was spent in wanderings through the mining regions where I expected to have to bring up at last—Previously I had not left San Francisco." No further statements seem available about his life from May until he went to the Southern Mines to join the "quartz excitement," which had been growing rapidly since the quieting of the Indians that spring at the end of the Mariposa "war." Of quartz mining and Indians let Sam Ward himself speak as "Midas, Jr."

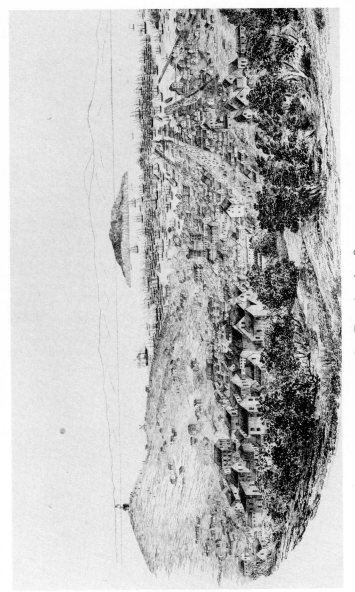

San Francisco in 1851

Incidents on
the "River of Grace"

By
MIDAS, JR.

IN THE SUMMER of 1851, I started from San Francisco with three friends, bent like myself upon inspecting some new and valuable "leads" of auriferous quartz recently uncovered in the vicinity of the town of Quartzburg and offered for sale, or participation in their profits, by the discoverers, who lacked the capital to render them productive. The respectability of these proprietors had inspired enough faith . . . . to induce quite a number of gentlemen of means to despatch us as a commission of scientific inquiry.

Business in San Francisco was shaping itself into the regular channels of trade; lots had reached their maximum, and speculation its apogee. The dry and river diggings had been pretty thoroughly washed and "rattled"; stories of colossal nuggets were becoming less frequent, and it was evident that the state must depend chiefly for its future yield of gold upon the mighty backbone of quartz rock, the abrasion and disintegration of which, by the wear and tear of ages, had enriched the *placers* with treasures exhausted by two years of Anglo-Saxon avidity. My associates were disposed to enter into a mining speculation with the *sang froid* of philosophers, and the prudence of political economists. They were prepared to lose their stake, but not to enlarge it. It was a lottery, wherein they took a ticket, and no more. All had become enriched by the lucrative speculations of the preceding two years, and quartz mining seemed likely to prove the next attractive branch of remunerative industry.

The new steamer *Sophie*, under the command of Lieut. Louis McLane, U.S.N., had just been launched upon the Stockton route, and leaving San Francisco at 4 o'clock P.M. for the moderate sum of ten dollars landed us at Stockton—distance a little more than a hundred miles —by daybreak of the following morn.[1] A couple of days were devoted to the friends who had colonized that town, whose promising prospects were already fading before the comparatively greater brilliance of the northern mines, to which Sacramento was owing its rapid growth. On the afternoon of the second day we were despatched by the kindness of Maj. Hammond, who had first laid out the town,[2] and become the partner of Captain Weber, its proprietor,[3] in a kind of *ambulance* to our first ferry, called Sirey's, on the Stanislaus River, some twenty-seven miles distant. We had hired four stout nags for the trip, and they followed us attached by "lariats" to the wagon. The ferryman, whose dwelling was an ale-house, received our visit with equal surprise and pleasure, travellers being scarce at that season of the year, when the shorter roads, higher up the stream, were practicable for teams; his being a winter ferry when, during the rainy season, the upper roads are almost impassable.[4] There was fortunately a

[1] The *Sophie* made her first trip to Stockton on August 12, 1851.

[2] Richard P. Hammond came to California in April 1849, on garrison duty. In June 1849 he finished surveying and mapping the site of Stockton for Charles Weber. In December 1850 he became Weber's partner.

[3] Charles M. Weber (1814–1881), a native of Hamburg, came to California overland in 1841. In 1844 he acquired the site of Stockton and soon began to give away lots to attract settlers. He discovered the first gold found in the Southern Mines, and his town rapidly grew to be the chief supply depot for that region.

[4] Sirey & Clark's advertisements, which began to appear in December of 1850, said their ferry was about five miles above the mouth

remainder of hay and barley sufficient for our animals; and for us the last two cans of oysters were produced at supper—our bedding, as a matter of course, being our blankets. On the morrow at daybreak, we forded the stream and followed a trail twenty miles to breakfast, which we obtained at the corresponding ferry upon the river Tuolumne. Having lost our way several times, it was nearly noon ere we broke our fast. We were duly ferried over and started for Belt's ferry upon the river Merced—a crossing known as "Howard's" in Mr. Hittel's life of Adams, the grizzly bear hunter.[5] The last stage of our journey was protracted until midnight. The track lay across a sandy plain with neither grass nor water; the sun was broiling hot, rendering this ride memorable as the occasion of one of the great . . . . Homeric thirsts of my existence . . . . having lost our way in the dark, we gave the horses the reins, and after a consultation among themselves, a snorting and a snuffing of the air, the intelligent brutes roused up to a livelier pace, advanced with increasing courage and celerity at right angles from the course we were pursuing, and brought us, in half an hour, to the bank of a broad and babbling river, where, for nearly an hour, we indulged in such potations as are unknown at the table of the *gourmet*. Having extinguished the fire that was consuming us, we mounted our steeds with gentle indications to them to carry us without delay to the nearest provender; and to our surprise they halted after a ten minutes' trot at the door of a hostelry

of the Stanislaus, and added that the "attention of travellers is particularly called to this route during the winter months, as the road is perfectly dry from the French camp to the Tuolumne, Mercede and Mariposa rivers."

[5] Theodore H. Hittel, *The Adventures of James Capen Adams, Mountaineer and Grizzly Bear Hunter, of California* (Boston and San Francisco, 1860).

called "Snelling's Ranche" where, having provided for our faithful pilots, we "turned in" around a hay stack, *sub Jove*.

A bright sun made sleep uncomfortable at an early hour in the morning . . . . so we arose, like Mr. Stephens' Yucatan nymph, "dressed for the day,"[6] and after a tolerably lively breakfast, we remounted, and set our faces toward Belt's ferry, some seven miles distant. Our way lay along the bank of the river; there was neither timber nor grass in sight, and the scene was a type of the barrenness and desolation of the *plateau* between the Merced and the Stanislaus during that dry season when neither rain nor dew for a period of six, and at times seven, months comforts the thirsty earth.

A tent, surrounded by a group of Indians, on a high bluff overlooking the river, and on the other side a narrow plain growing rapidly into hilly ground, brought us to a halt, and we learned that this was our crossing-place. Within the tent there was a small store, at the counter of which Indians were bartering gold dust, from quills and leather bags, for articles of necessity or luxury. One of our party had a slight previous acquaintance with Mr. Belt, the proprietor, who, upon being inquired for, received us with great cordiality. Little did I then dream that it would be my fate to pass in the small frame house upon the other side of the river the greater portion of the ensuing two years.

---

[6] John L. Stephens wrote *Incidents of Travel in Central America, Chiapas, and Yucatan* (New York, 1841); and *Incidents of Travel in Yucatan* (London, 1843).

THE FATIGUE resulting from our first experiment in the saddle, which had carried us over some fifty miles of country the day previous, and possibly the remnant of a small cask of very tolerable claret placed at our disposal (the mercury must have been at 90°), tempered our ardor to reach the Eldorado beyond and overcame our feeble resistance to the invitation to rest for a couple of days upon the "River of Grace." The name, too, sanctified by Catholic sympathies, seemed what the Latins call a *felix atque faustum omen* of our coming success. I am not prepared to assert that we should not have yielded to the same temptation on the shady banks of any cool river baptized after a less Christian calendar; but we really felt on the Merced like the *lazzaroni* sunning themselves in the porch of a church. Moreover, we had an opportunity of inspecting Indian life and manners, and what was more important, practical gold washing, for, on the afternoon of our arrival, the discovery of a new pocket attracted at least two hundred savages into the river, which was low enough in the broadest portion above the ferry to be forded waist deep. The scene was animated and picturesque, a *fusion* of the worships of the Baptist and the dancing Dervish of India, with a preponderance in costume towards the latter rite. The presence of both sexes, and of all ages, promiscuously kneeling in the river and huddled together with a wild and not inharmonious symmetry, gave the *coup d'oeil* a congregational aspect, and there were occasional

23

shouts of enthusiasm and satisfaction which would have made an impression even upon a Methodist camp meeting at white heat. A certain fascination held us spell-bound on the banks, and its interest was heightened by an acute curiosity to know what prizes were being drawn in this lottery of labor. Generally, the members of a wigwam kept together in their own watery pew; the father scooping into his *batea* the invisible mud and sand of the river bed, and the mother bearing it to the shore to perform those skillful gyratory manipulations by which the water is made to carry away from the shaken and rotated pan the earthy matter until after perhaps a hundred dippings and five times as many revolutions there remain at the bottom of the pan the yellow spangles surrendered by the

incongruous mass and now glittering upon an enamel of black sand. The precious metal was then gathered in a quill. . . . . With pick and crowbar, large boulders were occasionally dislodged from the sockets of ages as tenderly as his first-born removes the outer seal from the will of a millionaire.

Towards sunset the congregation retired and approached slowly, and with an air of coquettish indifference, the trading tent for the gew-gaws and flesh pots of which their hearts were languishing. As is the case in civilized life, they with the smallest purses were generally the earliest buyers, while those who had been more successful seemed really to enjoy emotions of transient avarice before parting with their gold. And in miniature this sensation was not incompatible with the customs of better educated humanity, which often halts in doubt whether to buy a shawl or a mantle, and sometimes ends with buying neither. If I remember aright, the average yield varied that afternoon from two to eight dollars a head; it was often less and rarely greater.

At dusk, fires began to glow in the distant *rancheria*, as Indian encampments are called, and we strolled down to it and trod its tortuous streets, pausing now and then to wonder at the relish with which they enjoyed their unenticing supper. The meat was cut in strips of a finger's thickness and toasted on sticks, each member of the family, from the gray ancestor down to the tottling urchin, officiating as his own Soyer.[1] The rustic character of the half-open hut, which, before its leaves were withered, resembled an improvised bower, the black hair and swarthy faces of the groups around the primitive *cuisine* in all, save the costume, reminded one of a gypsy camp, in which the important ingredient of a tea-kettle alone was wanting.

[1] Alexis Soyer (1809–1858), French cook.

We were not, apparently, regarded as intruders, although not invited to partake of their, to us, somewhat unsavory repast.

So far back as the month of August, 1849, I had seen in the hands of Col. Frémont several golden bullets which he had received (not in battle) as the result of the trituration and amalgamation with the mercury of the auriferous quartz[2] of his great Mariposa estate,[3] from which Belt's ferry was only twenty-five miles distant, the town of Quartzburg, our first destination, lying half way between that of Mariposa and our present quarters.

On the morning of the third day, we remounted, and

[2] Bayard Taylor, traveling as correspondent for the *New York Tribune*, also saw this gold, and wrote: "At the United States Hotel I again met with Colonel Frémont, and learned the particulars of the magnificent discovery which had just been made upon his ranche. . . . . It was nothing less than a vein of gold in the solid rock—the first which had been found in California. I saw some specimens which were in Col. Frémont's possession. The stone was a reddish quartz, filled with rich veins of gold, and far surpassing the specimens brought from North Carolina and Georgia. Some stones picked up on the top of the quartz strata, without particular selection, yielded two ounces of gold to every twenty-five pounds. . . . . This discovery made a great sensation throughout the country, at the time, yet it was but the first of many such."

[3] The Mariposa Grant, which dominated his later years, was one of the many confusing elements in the life of Frémont. In 1847 he gave the Monterey consul, Larkin, $3,000 to buy the Mexican title to a property near San Francisco; but Larkin bought the title to a large, distant tract vaguely located "within the limits of the Snow Mountains, the Merced, the Chauchilla and San Joaquin Rivers." In the period described by Sam Ward, the grant was claimed as indicated in the map on the end papers of this book, running for some distance along both sides of the Mariposa River. By the time court decisions of the middle 1850's gave Frémont a fairly clear title, he had abandoned claim to the agricultural land far down the Mariposa and claimed the mining area running north along the Great Johnson Lode to the Merced. The Mariposa Grant was then considered the world's most valuable piece of land owned by one man.

26

pursued our journey. We had scarcely gone a mile before the road began to mount the hills which slope thence for fifty miles, until lost in the snows of the Sierra Nevada. The timber grew larger as we ascended, though granite still controlled the region from the Merced to Quartzburg. In the incipient forest through which we passed there were few evidences of animal life; the magpie and grey quail being the only birds of the air, and an occasional rabbit dividing with the rattlesnake the empire of the earth. . . . . nothing can exceed in brilliancy of hue, or delicacy and grace of structure the myriads of [California flowers] which enamel its plains . . . .

The little town of Quartzburg lies at the termination of the spur of the first range of rising land which interrupts, towards the east, the plain of the San Joaquin River and its tributaries.[4] Nearly at the base of the hill we had just crossed, it overlooks a sloping plateau, terminating in the north at the Merced River, now some seven miles distant, and eastward in a fresh ascent of more vigorous and elevated hills, among which lay our path to Mariposa. A

[4] A letter from Quartzburg to the *Alta California* of October 24, 1851, described the town as it was not long after Sam Ward first knew it: "Quartzburg was formerly called Burns'. There are about a dozen large tents, most of them stores, one blacksmith's shop, a ten-pin alley, two boarding houses, and a number of unoccupied cabins. The camp is situated on Burns' Creek [which] was first worked in the winter of 1849, and then only a small portion of it, in the neighborhood of Quartzburg. Numbers of people settled here last Fall, but most of them, out of patience in waiting for rain, left for other diggings. Those who remained did well, and the greater portion of the creek has been worked with rockers. . . . . Most of the people here are engaged in quartz mining. Golden rocks are exhibited in every store, and quartz rock is the all-absorbing topic of conversation. The enterprising city of San Francisco is well represented here. Many of her merchant princes are deeply involved in the quartz mining business. I should judge that the prospect for quartz mining is better here than around Sonora and Big Oak Flat. The business, however, is in its infancy."

27

Texan pioneer, Col. Thorn, had erected on the summit of the knoll an old fashioned log cabin, with supplements of boards and shingles, in which the wayfarer found a well furnished store, a clean bunk, a tidy supper, with the luxury of milk, then a great rarity in all California, and abundant provender for his beasts. The Colonel had brought his slaves with him, and they had adhered to the fortunes of the Patriarch with unwavering fidelity. His wife was, to use a homely expression, "as good a woman as you meet anywhere," and I well remember that during my long exile below I used to regard a visit to Quartzburg very much as our Cuban neighbors do an excursion from broiling Havana, with its unalluring market (save to those who trade in sugar and tobacco), to the comfort, the luxury, and the refinement of that Mecca of modern *caravanserais*, the New York Hotel.[5]

Having come thus far for the purpose of inspecting the gold vein alluded to in the previous chapter, we quartered ourselves in "Thorn Villa," and devoted a day or two to the various "leads" and "outcroppings" of auriferous quartz which constitute the valley of Quartzburg. . . . .

[5] Thomas Thorn came to California in 1849 and like many others from Texas settled at the Southern Mines, the first gold area he came to. He was the leading citizen of Quartzburg and connected with much of its mining. He called and presided over the Mariposa Quartz Convention, which met at Quartzburg in June 1851 and established a code of rules for locating and retaining quartz claims which was satisfactory enough to be adopted in other parts of the Mother Lode, and was not changed in Mariposa until 1864. Courthouse records show that Colonel Thorn was a partner in at least sixteen veins in the neighborhood of Quartzburg, among them the Washington Vein and the Gaines Ledge. He was for a time president of a company operating the well-known Number Nine.

The one house still partially intact at Quartzburg is said to have been built by him. Local report also gives him credit for introducing opossum to the region.

The Washington vein,[6] which shortly after became our property, had already yielded highly remunerative returns to its discoverers,[7] who had worked it after the primitive Mexican fashion with *arrastres*, a slow but inexpensive process which may be compared to the grinding of corn by a single mill stone gliding in a circle over a series of smooth underlying rocks and pulled round by a mule harnessed to the end of the horizontal pole, at the middle of which it is suspended, the other end of the pole being fixed in a revolving shaft. This method, which certainly surpasses all others in the absorbing and searching thoroughness of its performance, seems a waste of time when compared with the more considerable results to be attained by machinery. And yet there are many material pursuits in which the calculations of the "rule of three," however earnestly applied, far from justify the professed accuracy of that arithmetical proportion. Davenport's Electro-Magnetic Machine, which threatened to convert the Aurora Borealis

[6] This vein, which was discovered in 1850, proved rich, producing before the end of the century about two million dollars worth of gold, and that by the most wasteful methods. The vein averaged twelve feet in width, and by 1881 the 1,600-foot shaft was famous as the deepest in California. Although the property often has changed hands and often has been shut down, it always has been among the three or four most consistently worked in the Quartzburg-Mariposa region. Today it is joined with the Franklin and Jenny Lind veins as the Jenny Lind Mine.

[7] The first quartz taken out in 1850 by the discoverers of the Washington Vein came from a "chimney of very rich ore" and when worked by *arrastres* yielded "about $100 per ton." The owners, two months before Sam Ward's visit of inspection, had finished assembling a stamp mill which came from Georgia. One of the partners, writing to a Stockton paper in July of 1851, said it "repeatedly turned out over *one thousand dollars a day*." But the primitive machinery, though perhaps suitable enough for the gold-bearing ores of Georgia, soon broke down on California quartz and sent the local owners to San Francisco in search of the capital to build a better mill.

An *arrastre*

into a locomotive power some twenty years ago,[8] as well as Professor Ericsson's more recent appropriation of atmospheric air for the same purpose,[9] are instances of its fallacy; but nowhere is the illusion so painfully dispelled as by the calculation, "if a quintal of quartz rock ground and amalgamated in an *arrastre* yields ten dollars of pure gold, the product of a ton of ore must be two hundred and twenty dollars, and the result of a steam mill capable of crushing fifty tons a day will be eleven thousand dollars, say three hundred thousand dollars a month. And in a year of three hundred working days, three millions of dollars."

Our proposed purchase had certainly an attractive appearance; the rock was friable, and when pulverized in

[8] Thomas Davenport, of Vermont, built and displayed an electric automobile about 1835.

[9] John Ericsson, a Swedish-American, had invented several engines by the time Ward wrote—and the next year was to design the *Monitor*.

the iron mortar and its dust washed in the Mexican horn spoon, the "color of gold" was always manifested in the result. The proprietors, who were residents of the town of Quartzburg, had offered us one-half the mine for fourteen thousand dollars, to be expended in machinery for its development.[10] We closed the bargain with a stipulation that the "prospect" of the lead should prove satisfactory to an old Chilean miner who had once been the *capataz* of similar works in his native country.[11] There were seventeen other veins besides the Washington, which ran like the ribs of a gridiron from Quartzburg to the Merced River. It is said that when a stranger goes to Kentucky to buy a thoroughbred colt . . . . the owners of the various studs draw lots who shall have the first dash at him; nothing can be more loyal than their fidelity to this compact. The animal which may chance to take the purchaser's eye is pronounced by all, without a qualification or even a sinister shrug, the faultless nonpareil of the country, and so of the next one which may engage the buyer's attention; but when the sale has been consummated, the new comer finds numbers of unbought animals far superior to the one upon which he has laid out his money. So it was in Quartzburg; while the negotiation was pending, the Washington was worth all the veins in Mariposa put together, but when it had changed hands, or rather halves, it was surprising how much richer "leads" had been withheld from our knowledge through motives of delicacy towards the worthy angler who had netted us in San Francisco.

[10] A full list of the local shareholders is not available, but various sources show that prominent among them were Thomas Thorn, James M. McVicar, and Thomas C. Flournoy. Among the San Francisco acquaintances of Sam Ward who were to buy into the mine were E. Woodruff, A. B. Eaton, and Captain Erasmus Keyes.

[11] Chileans were among the first gold seekers to arrive in California.

Having concluded our *negocio*, we passed a day or two in examining the other seventeen candidates for the enterprise of speculative capitalists, and found all of them attractive and one or two quite enticing. They were (with one exception, the "Gaines ledge," which was the property of an elder brother of the illustrious General and was, properly speaking, a *manta*, or flat breadth of rock without depth)[12] sharp ribs of outcropping quartz rock, lying in a northwesterly direction. . . . . It was singular that these ledges, in almost every instance, had yielded from their very apices extremely rich specimens, either of gold in the shape of roots or branches, as though deposited there by a crystalline process, or honey-combing the rock in such yellow abundance that it seemed the promise of a *gold vein sprinkled with quartz*. These surface manifestations, however, did not endure a deeper penetration; and one would almost have fancied that they were samples ostentatiously paraded by nature to catch the eye of avarice. Our inspection gave a clue to the motives of the Quartzburg proprietors, who, having first exhausted these accessible fat ores and found the quartz imbued with fine and almost impalpable particles of gold only to be evoked by science and machinery, now called in the aid of that power to which both matter and intelligence are tributary.

From Quartzburg we started for Mariposa, some twelve or fifteen miles distant, via Bear Valley, then the scene of the incipient, and intended gigantic, operations

[12] The Gaines Ledge was discovered on September 21, 1850, by P. Hussey, a Texan, who later claimed it was the second vein discovered "in the South, with the exception of the Frémont vein at Mariposa." In October 1851 the claim was worked by a company of thirteen members who included "J. & E. Gaines," the former presumably the John B. Gaines who had been active in the Mariposa Quartz Convention during June of that year. The "illustrious General" to whom Ward referred was Edmund Pendleton Gaines (1777–1849).

of "The Merced Mining Company," which subsequently under the more cosmopolitan title of "The Nouveau Monde" decoyed the sovereigns of John Bull from his capacious pockets[13] and might, with the skillful manipulations of a second Law (George[14] or John[15]), have revived the extinct rages of the *Rue Quincampoix*. We were joined by that amiable and experienced peripatetic, Mr. Lippincott, generally known in this state as "Old Lip," not from any personal antiquity but because one of the "oldest inhabitants" of a state not two years old.[16]

[13] In the spring of 1851 the Merced Mining Company was formed to work the Great Johnson Lode. It built large reduction works at Mount Ophir, but results proved so poor that in January 1852 it stopped operations.

The Nouveau Monde Company, capitalized in England for $500,-000, leased mining rights in Bear Valley from Frémont's London agent. When its representatives arrived in California they found Frémont's title to his grant uncertain; so in May 1852 they bought from the inoperative Merced Mining Company a ten-year lease of its holdings. The Nouveau Monde found operations unprofitable and quit early in 1854.

In 1855 the Merced Mining Company resumed operations, but was hardly under way when the courts approved Frémont's claim to the mineral rights along the Great Johnson Lode. From then on the company operated mostly in lawsuits.

[14] George Law (1806–1881), New York promoter of railroads, steamship lines, and city transit systems.

[15] John Law (1671–1729), created a French speculative mania centering about the Rue Quincampoix, then a bourse.

[16] Benjamin S. Lippincott (1815–1870) came overland to California in an immigrant train which traveled for a time with the Donners. According to one of the members of the train, he was badly wounded by a poisoned arrow at the Humboldt; but he arrived at Sutter's Fort well enough to volunteer for Frémont's battalion at the end of October 1846. In 1848 he settled in Stockton and became active in politics, being a representative at the 1849 constitutional convention and serving for a time in the state senate. The *Stockton Times* frequently referred to his good nature and the pleasure others took in his

Our first taste of genuine mountain travel commenced with our ascent of Bear Mountain, which encloses the western edge of this valley of the same name. The trail was steep and disagreeable to climb and frightful to descend, but the scenery exhibited a certain semi-Alpine grandeur, and the valley itself was no tame counterpart of Vallombrosa. At the bottom of the mountain, our path lay beneath the shade of magnificent pines, and here and there a dark brook refreshed our steeds and imparted to the meadows a verdure which had not met our eyes for several days. Nothing could be more romantic than the site of the Bear Mountain tent, in a "plantation" of *manzanita* bushes couching under the shadow of towering "red woods." We here met Mr. Richard Killaly, the Pizarro of this new Peru, under whose energetic and experienced hands it was contemplated to erect Cyclopian forges, destined to convert into bar gold the walls of quartz rock which unconsciously enclosed the eastern portion of the valley.

. . . . I remember Mr. Killaly as the Evangelist from whom I first learned the mining creed in San Francisco, where, in a small tenement on Montgomery Street, he was wont to hold forth upon the availability of auriferous quartz, and to illustrate it by such alluring practical examples of its pulverization in the iron mortar and levigation in the horn spoon as made the mouths of his hearers fairly water with the *auri sacra fames.* The success which attended his preachings suggested the inquiry to what extent Peter the Hermit employed the treasures of the infidel as an incitement for the redemption of the Holy Sepulchre.

We therefore gladly delayed our journey to witness

---

company. With Thomas Thorn, A. H. Sibley, and Joseph Tivy—all friends of Sam Ward—Lippincott very early in 1851 located a claim near Quartzburg.

the laying of the corner stone of this colossal scheme and to examine, under the guidance of its projector, the rocky fortress which he was about to sack and the siege materials placed at his disposal.

It would require the pen of a Walter Scott to delineate the brilliant type of a mining Dalgetty[17] in full campaign which Mr. Killaly presented on that memorable evening devoted to the discussion of his plans for the subjection of the arch enemy Quartz. His name is a sufficient index of his nativity, and after having undergone the discipline of Trinity College, Dublin, he had received his spurs, not from the renowned Gustavus Adolphus, but from the immortal Lampadius, the superintendent of the great mining school of Freiberg, Saxony, to whom the scientific world is indebted for the discovery of that asymptote of the diamond—the carburet of sulphur.[18] From Freiberg, his diploma had procured him a commission under the seal of some English mining company, as an employee in their corps at Zacatecas, Mexico, where he had been engaged during seventeen years in extracting silver, with fortunes varying with the richness of the mines to which they were attached. His presence in California was, perhaps, an evidence of the exiguity of recent dividends, although the rising state numbered, particularly from the west coasts of our continent, emigrants of large wealth; which I mention to show that avarice quite as often as poverty was the multiplying power of our population. Our host's conversation was a rich and jovial medley, unfolded in German, Spanish, Latin, Irish, and even English, in which his principal object seemed to be to mask under a *feu de joie* of learning and pleasantry the categorical development of

[17] Captain Dugald Dalgetty, a soldier of fortune in Scott's *Legend of Montrose.*

[18] Wilhelm August Lampadius (1772–1842).

35

his plans, calculations, and *bona fide* expectations. No Irish free-lancer whose pennon had waved for seventeen years in Mexico could be suspected of mendicancy, but Mr. Killaly displayed unsurpassed ingenuity in *begging the question* when he could not elude it. But more of this worthy *condottiere* hereafter.[19]

We devoted the morrow to the examination of Bear Valley, which is nine miles in length, and has its throat cut by the Merced River, deep, narrow and impetuous. The great eastern wall of quartz, which rises abruptly on the left of the road to Mariposa, runs directly to the river, where it evidently was severed by a convulsion of nature. The side of the fissure on the left bank of the stream exhibits strata, and also irregularities, corresponding so minutely with the formation of the rock opposite that the eye sees at a glance that if again clapped together the two sections would reunite with the accuracy of the corresponding halves of a severed plum cake. . . . .

---

[19] Richard Griffith Killaly (? 1805–1859), Fellow of the Royal Geological Society, came to Bear Valley to inspect the Great Johnson Lode. He found it rich and recommended the formation of the Merced Mining Company to acquire it from its locator. Killaly was one of the partners in the newly formed company, and in charge of much of its operation. For a time maps gave his name to the ridge running along the eastern side of Bear Valley.

THE MINING regions were full of . . . . ardent and untaught youths of mature age who had added to our English vocabulary the significant verb "to prospect," and it was by one of these, surnamed "Quartz Johnson,"[1] that I was torn from the meditative embrace of Killaly and conducted over rugged peaks of moss-covered rock to the top of a mountain, where, although none of the kingdoms of earth was in view, I was assured by that golden enthusiast that its richest treasures lay beneath our feet. An opium eater, or a devotee of hashish, might well have envied that worthy the gorgeous dreams which dimmed the sun and illumined the night of his existence. Light and wiry of frame, long of limb, swift of foot, and chested like a greyhound, he might have commanded the "phantom bark" in Moore's ballad. If "knowledge is power" and wealth one of its concomitants, "Quartz Johnson" was a Socrates, an Alexander, and a Rothschild; like the former, he was willing to impart what he knew, and unlike the latter, to share his empire and his opulence. You could have one-half of any of his three hundred "veins," would you supply machinery and labor to work the other. In

[1] In 1850 John F. Johnson discovered the Great Johnson Lode, running from Horseshoe Bend on the Merced south to Mount Ophir. When the Merced Mining Company acquired his right to the Lode in March 1851, it made him one of the company's board of five trustees. In 1873 the *Mariposa Gazette*, in a retrospective article bravely entitled "The First Quartz Mill in California," said that during 1850 Johnson built two quartz mills, one run by horse power, the other by steam.

37

his log-hut lay classified, with a certain rude method, scores of bags and heaps of ores in newspapers, each labelled with some hieroglyphic, which only revealed to the proprietor the position of the cave "*sesame*" where it was to be found. This Croesus-errant seemed to have large transactions with the acute Killaly.

For, to do the latter justice, he possessed an intimate knowledge of all the recondite subtleties of assaying by the "dry method," and, besides being a practiced metallurgist, Freiburg, Lampadius, and Mexican experience had impressed him with no mean perception of mineralogical geology. Modesty has rarely been the barrier to a Celt's preferment, and it would have been unjust to himself to have hid his light under a bushel, or to have diminished its radiance among the eager but benighted votaries of Plutus who surrounded him. Like the barrister who was always puzzled to comprehend his client's statement of his case until magnified by a cheque, he uniformly manifested a "profound doubt" as to the value of a specimen until, like a conscientious scholiast, he could examine the context. It was in vain that Johnson would assure him that such an ore came from some inaccessible peak, to which it would require the cords and pulleys of an eiderdown hunter to hoist his rotund and inagile proportions. The adept was inexorable until either the locality was shown, or a certain buckskin bag, filled with some of the more agreeable reminiscences of Mr. Johnson's hammer, was opened, and a share of its contents imparted to the philosopher.

Next to the people who thus trade in information come those who have the means of buying it. These two classes, together with the brawny delvers and the extortionate shop and tavern keepers, constitute the population of a mining region. Our party was embraced in the second of the categories and [was] indebted to Mr. Johnson for an amount of exercise that would have wearied the limbs of a professional deer-stalker. We left the valley without having made a purchase, but with the assurance to our mining cicerone that we would recommend him and his discoveries to our rich friends below.

From Bear Valley to Mariposa, some seven or more miles, the trail gradually crept up thicker clusters of hills and then dropped us into a sloping valley, which wound round the foot of a more considerable elevation. Above and around us the scenery in rock and forest increased in grandeur, but our path at the bottom lay over the dividing walls of square pits, from eight to ten feet deep, and about the same width, which had yielded their contents to the pan or the cradle of the miner. The approach to a manufacturing town is heralded by cinders and scoria, and that of a mining city is as honeycombed as though the lids of all the huge tombs of the *Campo-Santo* at Naples, three hundred and sixty-five in number, should be simultaneously uncovered.

In Bear Valley we had witnessed little or no mining proper; in Mariposa we saw nothing else. By mining proper I do not imply its meaning at the School of Freiberg or in the hills of Guanajuato but the extraction of ores by pick, crowbar and shovel, and their immediate levigation in the cradle or the pan. It was no longer the joyous multitude we had beheld digging, washing and screaming in the Merced River and then emerging like butterflies or grasshoppers from the store; but the tough labor of one or, at most, two sallow and bearded white men in the same pit, dislodging obstinate boulders and scraping with knives the unctuous mud from the interstices in joints and strata of slate; the ring of the crowbar, and the sharp twang of the pick. But few panfuls of earth rewarded their daily toil, but, oh! how carefully these were "washed out" in the puddled waters of the narrow creek which mean-

39

dered the Valley. These were what are termed "dry diggings," and the gold was coarse, silver its principal alloy, and its value from three to five dollars an ounce less than the purer metal of the "river diggings."

There were some distinguished strangers at the principal hotel. An Oxford scholar with his wife, a handsome English lady of refreshing aspect, had come out with a staff of engineers and some half-score of Cornish miners to take possession of certain veins believed in and bought by an English company from a dexterous mining peddler who had carried to London an eclectic cabinet of rich specimens of California ores at the time of "the Great Exhibition," and had very cleverly located them in a particular vein belonging to himself, which he had been persuaded to dispose of.[2] The friends and partners of this expert negotiator had secured one or two leads of meagre quartz on the hillside back of Mariposa which did not appear to realize the sanguine anticipations of this mining commission. Our party gladly fraternized with the heads of the expedition, more particularly with the mining captains, who were men of experience in Cornish metallurgy . . . . thus far, few practical experts of that description had made their appearance in the Golden State.[3] It was true that their knowledge of the business had hitherto been confined to the tin, copper, and lead deposits of the English Duchy; but in their case, the "rule of three" previously alluded to was likely to hold good, and even should it not

---

[2] Ward possibly referred to George W. Wright, who displayed quartz samples in the Crystal Palace when the Great Exhibition opened in 1851.

[3] The "Oxford scholar" whom Ward met was not the first representative of English capital to bring Cornish miners to California. Several accompanied Sir Henry Vere Huntly, of the Anglo-California Gold Mining Company, when he visited Mariposa in the autumn of the previous year.

turn out that men skillful in pursuing a vein of tin should be, *a fortiori*, susceptible of following and developing a lead of gold, they would probably have better success than miners whose spades and picks had never penetrated much deeper than the bed of a potato patch. What particular information of value I derived from these adepts has now escaped me; but I know of no better place than the present in which to record that during a sojourn of some five years in California I never knew an instance of the success either of professors, with diplomas as broad as our liberties, or of practical miners from the old world, with shoulders as broad as said diplomas.[4] It was not only a new state and a new order of things in the moral but also in the physical world, for never, previously, had from fifty to one hundred thousand men assembled without a viceroy or an army, much less without a government, as in California, to appropriate to themselves, by the democratic right of the strongest, the virgin treasures of the earth; and I may as well add that human experience, as digested in books, gave no clue to the mysterious golden labyrinths of its hills and valleys.

The town of Mariposa, in the year of grace 1851, was the *ultima Thule* of the so-called "Southern Mines."[5]

[4] But one group of Cornish miners seems to have done fairly well if trust can be put in the report by the *San Joaquin Republican* of November 15, 1851, that on the previous Thursday twelve of them "who dug to a depth of 60 feet below the surface, at the rear of the United States Hotel [in Sonora,] struck a vein of quartz literally full of gold."

And Sam Ward overlooked the fact that in 1850 Cornish miners, because of their experience in the Old World, were the first to deduce the presence of the rich Tertiary gravels.

[5] The Southern Mines were variously defined as the part of the Mother Lode region that was south of the Cosumnes River, or that was south of the "ridge on the north side of the North Fork of the Mokelumne."

There were, to be sure, filaments of gold farther south, reaching to the Fresno, but these were but small fibres from the root of the mighty tree whose stem and branches have since been found as high as the Cascade Mountains of Oregon, and as broadly spread as the auriferous sands of Frazer's River. No traveller makes a long stay at Falmouth (Land's End), since the days in which the late Mr. Beckford was detained there a week or more, waiting for a fair wind to conduct him to Lisbon;[6] and we pursued the same course with regard to Mariposa, whence we hastened back to Quartzburg, paying on our way a flying visit to Mr. Killaly. We found this gentleman occupied, until the heavy machinery of his reduction works should arrive, with opening ledge upon ledge and Pelion upon Ossa of quartz, and testing their yellow promises of fortune at the bottom of his inseparable horn spoon. By the side of his little cabin, a Mexican *peon* who had followed his fortunes from Zacatecas seemed eternally busied in crushing with a colossal crowbar fresh specimens of quartz, in a mortar from which a tolerably large bombshell might have been projected. In the collection of rocks which formed the basis of these experiments the same show of classification was observable as in the worthy adept's cabinet in San Francisco. In truth, the house of his faith was built upon the rock and not the sand, and when the enthusiasm of his associates paled, or their faith flagged, he was always ready to revive their hopes and even to repel skepticism with a fresh revelation of the golden evangel.

Should this narrative prove palatable to the epicures of this journal, I shall hereafter trace, perhaps dimly, perhaps in clear outline, the vivid contrasts of light and shade, the after history, the decline and fall of these mutable empires of wealth . . . . all these schemes and

[6] William Beckford, in March 1787.

undertakings with their failures or successes are but repetitions upon a grand or diminutive scale of the great crusade of the nineteenth century, in which Baron Rothschild plays the part of Peter the Hermit. The chronicles of the Golden Gate would doubtless contain lessons as instructive as any genuine legions[7] of human suffering or human joy. The goddess who is said to reside at the bottom of a well, if not always stranger than fiction, is at times quite as interesting; and while the world has already felt the material influence of its accession of Australian[8] and Californian gold, it may be years before human society realizes the moral effect of these unexpected inheritances of wealth by proletarian communities, now amounting to more than a million of souls.

Our friends at Quartzburg, who had witnessed our departure for the seductive Lotus Isles of fairy Mariposa, manifested sincere delight at our return without bushels of rival quartz ores in our saddle bags and without having transferred our affections or our cupidity to regions more famous than their modest valley. It was a decided triumph for them that our eyes and hearts should not have yielded to the temptations which must doubtless have been spread before us, and every proprietor of mining veins went to bed that night from twenty-five to fifty per cent richer than he had arisen in the morning.

We left the little town which our presence had thus gladdened at daylight, purposing to break our fast at Belt's and to push on to Stockton, where we were due the following afternoon. Whether the game of "draw" had been protracted beyond the small hours, or that Captain Tivy, the aid-de-camp of Colonel Thorn,[9] was an early riser, he

[7] Legends?   [8] Gold was discovered at New South Wales in 1852.

[9] Joseph A. Tivy was associated with Colonel Thorn in a large number of mining ventures. He also located some claims independently of Thorn, sometimes as J. A. Tivy & Company. With Thorn he was

stood by to speed our parting with a glass of old Virginia "peach and honey," which still awakens tingling reminiscences in the region of the brain. I do not remember a more pleasant ride than our gallop of that morning, unless, perhaps, the last quarter upon the road to Cruces (before the construction of the Panama Railroad), with its "palaces" in sight and its fleet of "bungos" dancing attendance in the Chagres River upon the homeward bound California passengers in the years '49 and '50. If the "peach and honey" at that early hour of the morning savored of impropriety or intemperance, I shall leave the defence of that tipple to Mr. Lippincott, whose sagacity and experience pronounced it indispensable on that peculiar arc of the earth's meridian; at all events, it, or our nags, brought us in fine spirits to the ferry, where we were greeted with news of no little interest to its proprietors. The Indians had made a "ten strike," having fallen in with an undiscovered pocket in the bend of the river from which they had taken several thousand dollars since our departure. The shelves of the store were "cleaned out"; it was impossible to get up a new wagon load of goods from Stockton in less than a week, and it was feared that in the interval the improvident nabobs might, in their eagerness to convert their dust into more desirable objects, transfer their allegiance to rival trading posts in the vicinity. I had the honor of being consulted upon this question of mingled ethics and political economy, and recommended the sacrifice of

---

one of the partners in the Quartzburg Mining Company, which in September 1850 located nine veins, among them the Texas, later called the Number Nine.

In 1851 he made a map of Quartzburg and the gold-bearing veins in its neighborhood to which there is frequent reference in early quartz claims. In July 1852 he became Surveyor in the first group of officers elected upon the formation of Tulare County.

a small herd of cattle belonging to the establishment at reduced rates to tempt the gluttons of the tribe, a suggestion which was adopted with eminent success. . . . . the apprehended calamity was averted, and the little store preserved its customers. The day of our arrival also witnessed our departure, and under the guidance of Mr. Belt, who was hastening down for the desired supplies, we made a forced march to Stockton of over sixty miles within ten hours.

It is needless here to recapitulate by what process of reasoning or negotiation one of my companions, who had already taken an interest in the Quartzburg vein, was led to "buy into" the Merced store and ferry; perhaps with a view to have two strings to his bow, and not to put all his eggs in one basket. At first sight, this setting off of golden sand against golden quartz . . . . was a clever "hedge" on the betting book of one interested in the race of fortune. [10]

Let it suffice here to say that on our return to San

[10] This friend who bought into George G. Belt & Company, operators of the store and ferry, was Henry Drought, of San Francisco, listed in directories of 1852–53 as a real estate dealer with the same Dupont Street address as Sam Ward's former partner, Price. Before Drought became involved with the establishment on the Merced it had had a simple history. Late in 1850 Thomas Howard and a partner bought the ferry. In April 1851 Thomas Howard became sole owner and advertised the property for sale, calling it by its old name, the California Ranch Crossing. When George Belt was licensed as an Indian trader the next month, he took over a share of the Merced property, forming Belt & Company with his brother, Upton H. Belt, and Thomas Howard and his brother, William J. Howard, as partners. The company then built a similar establishment on the Tuolumne.

It was near the beginning of September 1851 that Drought joined the company. As one might assume from Sam Ward's phraseology, the venture did not turn out well financially for his friend; in fact, it ruined him.

Francisco a company was duly organized to go into operation so soon as Don Gregorio, the Chilean expert already
alluded to, should inspect our proposed purchase and report a favorable verdict. I found this veteran *capataz*
lying *perdu* with a friend and countryman, who was herd-
ing cattle and growing cabbages on a fragment of the
Peralta *ranche* at Contra Costa, which I reached one morning at sunrise in a wherry. Don Santiago Arcos had supplied me with a passport to his confidence, which roused
him from his slumbers. Our bargain was made upon a
raw hide, cemented with a cup of coffee, and sanctified by
the calumet of a cigarito. A small bundle, containing an
extra flannel shirt, a hammer, a chisel, a horn spoon and
a magnifying glass, constituted my new friend's outfit,
and on the same afternoon the dashing little *Sophie* conveyed us again to Stockton. In two days we reached
Quartzburg, and Don Gregorio, with a couple of stout
navvies at his disposal, set to work upon his investigations
of the golden quarry out of which we all hoped to rear
the edifices of future fortunes. The proprietors, though
in some little suspense, manifested no apprehension as to
the result of his researches. A day or two convinced them
that he was a "workman" in his calling, and from the
neighborhood quite a number of "prospectors" thronged to
Thorn Villa to induce the mining sage to examine their
discoveries. Having engaged him for "so much the round
trip," I felt no scruple in farming out his experience to
the uninitiated at a rate which covered not only the stipulated remuneration but also the cost of our journey.

Don Gregorio formed a highly favorable opinion of
our vein. The purchase was consummated, and in less than
a month I found myself located upon the River of Grace,
where I proposed to remain a year or more and see the
hands played out which had been dealt to my friend in

the double game of Indian trading at the river and of quartz crushing near the village.[11]

It is, perhaps, an incentive to the perusal of the great serials of the day, that no reader can take a peep at their conclusion and anticipate the *dénouement*. What was the result of this dual speculation may hereafter be confided to the curious reader.

These columns are proof that "I still live" but are no index of the degree in which these enterprises prospered or diminished my worldly fortunes. I was weary of civilization, which was already fast encroaching upon the Bohemian structure, or rather want of structure, of San Francisco society, and gladly accepted the proposal of this contemplated hiatus in an existence of nearly thirty years of unwearied activity, varied by such lights and shades of good and bad fortune as had rarely fallen to the lot of a person of sufficient education if not to safely navigate his bark through the reefs and quicksands of life, at all events to take a sight of sun, moon or stars and work up his reckoning at any hour of the day or night. On the River of Grace, there would be no cupboards for my skeletons to hide in; and as for phantoms, I had dealt so largely in the unsubstantial that they could no longer impair my fortunes. Most lovers of narratives of travel will remember how, from the days of Robinson Crusoe down to those of Dr. Livingstone, their fancy has occasionally been captivated by some sketch from "still life" of a seclusion and repose which seemed enviable, whether among the ruins of Palenque, or beneath the mysterious arches of

---

[11] In one of the few letters that he wrote from California, Sam Ward told his sister, Julia Ward Howe, that he had settled at Belt's on September 10, 1851. His duties, as he testified in a lawsuit many years later, were a "general superintendence of the purchases of cattle and flour, a fatherly care of the Indians . . . . and keeping Drought who lived in San Francisco advised of what was going on at the ferry."

A miner, by Charles Nahl

Petra, on the banks of the Great Fish River, or beneath the palms of Typee. Such a life without a post-office I was about to essay among the Indians—a life in the open air, with Horace to teach me philosophy, Virgil pastoral delights, and the varied luck of the dusky gold diggers around me the inconstancy if not the worthlessness of fortune.

The little frame house on the river was to be my Albanian Villa, and Quartzburg my future Rome, where the only affairs of state and rumors of war were the yield of the neighboring mines and the success of the "last blast." In addition to these attractive novelties, my attention would be interested in the progress of the solution of our little share in the great quartz problem, which might possibly, though my expectations never ran me into debt, enhance with the pleasures of solid success the meditative joys of this voluntary exile.

In this view, I was settled down in a day with an abundant supply of coffee and tobacco, the great solaces of the recluse, and a lot of choice tea and sugar, the absence of which, in the reports of the American Board of Foreign Missions, seems to constitute the principal grief of their diplomatic corps. Though lumber was worth four hundred dollars per thousand feet, I indulged in the luxury of a small table; an old friend had given me a brass bedstead at starting; and my last surplus funds had been expended upon a Mexican saddle and bridle of some little distinction. What cared I for money when I was about to walk and sleep on golden sands? and was I not still vigorous enough, if needed, to go into the river, dredge my own mud and wash out my own pan?

THAT accomplished traveller and persevering hunter, the late Mr. Ruxton, in the narrative of his trip through Mexico to the Rocky Mountains, dwells, with tender longings and heartfelt regrets, upon his sojourn for the period of several weeks in the seclusion of a grassy nook near the "Beer or Soda Springs," sheltered by the Wind River Mountains, where he enjoyed the luxury of absolute solitude, diverted only by the custody and purveyance of his animals, and enlivened by the sports of the chase. . . . .[1]

The tranquillity which pervaded the region of my retirement, although not so unbroken as that of Mr. Ruxton's retreat, so far from proving irksome, was refreshing in its repose to one who had just quitted the carnival excitement of San Francisco existence. Such a rustication kept one out of mischief and avoided, if it did not cover like charity, foreign or domestic, a multitude of sins. There were no unsaleable goods to be "worked off"; I say this feelingly, having once paid the freight upon a consignment of obsolete stoves, which I was unable to *give* away. There were no "steamer days," calling for heavy remittances from an exhausted treasury and an estate mortgaged beyond capital temptation; no fever from the

[1] George Frederick Ruxton (1820–1848), a British officer whose travels in the West have not received all the attention they deserve, described this sojourn in chapter xxviii of his *Adventures in Mexico and the Rocky Mountains* (London, 1847).

infection of "good things," as new speculations in coals, sugars, rice, flour, lots, and especially occult Mexican titles to the latter, were then called; no gnashing regrets when the unexpected success of some enterprise which you had scorned as worthless had proved your neighbor as wise as you were foolish, an unclassified weakness of human nature—call it emulation, envy, or avarice—which leads mankind to more than half their griefs. . . . .

The dividends my friend expected to derive from his investment at Belt's *ranche* were to be earned by the tolls of the ferry, the profits of the Indian store, and the gains upon a contract, entered into with the U.S. Indian sub-agent for that section, to furnish the Merced and Tuolumne tribes with certain supplies of flour and fresh meat as inducements for their tranquillity and for their abstinence from depredations upon the cattle and horses of their white neighbors.[2]

The business of the ferry, though never swollen by unexpected tides of emigration attracted to the Southern

[2] On March 19, 1851, near the end of the Mariposa "war," six tribes signed a treaty—which, along with seventeen similar California treaties, the United States Senate never ratified and kept secret for decades. The treaty granted the six tribes a reservation between the Merced and the Tuolumne, as shown in the map on the end papers of this book. In the treaty the names of the tribes appeared as Si-yan-te, Po-to-yun-te, Co-co-noon, Apang-as-se, Aplache, A-wal-a-che. They acknowledged United States jurisdiction and gave up all right to the land of California outside the reservation. The government agreed to protect them and teach them useful arts. Instead of annual gifts of money in perpetuity as in many earlier treaties made to the east, the government promised that during 1851 and 1852 it would give the six tribes jointly a hundred head of beef and a hundred sacks of flour each year.

When three United States commissioners arrived to treat with the Indians, George Belt visited them and made such a good impression that they named their next camp after him. Later, in May 1851, as Belt & Company, he received an exclusive license to trade with the six tribes

Mines by rumors of "rich strikes" and of "monster nuggets," was sufficiently uniform to pay the wages of the white "help" employed on the premises. Indeed, the boat and its appointments were of an inexpensive description. At its average height, the river was some eighty yards wide; a cable about fifty fathoms long had been stretched across and fastened to a couple of trees which grew opportunely on either bank; two sliding slings at the bow and stern of the boat were thrown over the cable, and the ferryman drew the boat across by hauling upon it. The boat was just large enough to hold a loaded six-mule wagon, and a stout boy could work the whole affair with ease. The teams generally arrived towards nightfall, and our whole establishment was thrown into a bustle of delight when a procession of half a dozen or more wagons loomed from the opposite bank. Their appearance early in the afternoon was wont to inspire the apprehension of their continuing their journey after crossing, but when the day was far advanced preparations might be safely made for their lodging and supper, and they were looked upon as sure customers for both, though upon the excellence of the latter might depend their stopping for breakfast; and this reminds me that I had forgotten to mention that the so-called store was, like all similar establishments in the mines, a hostelry for the nonce.

The late Mr. Becquerel,[3] whose brilliant discoveries

---

living on the Merced-Tuolumne reservation. Belt & Company later contracted to furnish to those tribes the beef and flour stipulated in the treaty.

The first two tribes listed above set up their *rancheria* on Belt & Company's land, just across the Merced River from their reservation; the other four settled on the Tuolumne at the store managed for the company by William J. Howard, one of the partners.

[3] This is presumably a reference to Antoine César Becquerel, although at the time Ward wrote the French physicist was still alive, aged seventy-three.

have so greatly enriched the treasury of electrical science, performed most of his experiments on a minute scale, chiefly in watch glasses; and had I been ambitious of putting to shame the unwieldy, sometimes incomprehensible, and often contradictory prolusions of Smith, Say, Storch, Ricardo, and other political economists, I have no doubt that the fluctuations of the trade of our little store at the ferry would have enabled me to lay down the basis and prove the developments of their much vexed science with a truth of premise, a simplicity of argument, and an irresistibility of conclusion which would forever have set at rest the disputes that still agitate the "money and trade articles" of our day.

Unlike most producers, whether by agricultural industry or by manufactures, our market lay under our eyes; the demand depended not upon political caprice nor upon wars and the other contingencies of national good or bad fortune but upon the success of our consumers in their gold washings. If their labors, which were under our constant supervision, had been richly rewarded, all hands were needed in the store; were they lazy or dispirited by two or three days of bad luck, it was haunted only by the loafers and beggars of the tribe, and occasionally honored by the visit of one of its few economical capitalists who was sure, in those times of commercial inactivity, to drive a good bargain.

The question of profits upon the beef and flour contract, though at first sight as alluring as a new mining prospectus, was more problematic if not mythical. Uncle Sam, though good for what he puts his name to, is as dilatory and scrutinizing of all bills not yet accepted as the veriest Bohemian that ever questioned the items or postponed the payment of a tailor's account. In our case, the supplies were honestly furnished, the accounts made out with scrupulous exactitude by that most prudish, squeamish, and methodical of honest book-keepers,[4] Judge Stakes,[5] whilom of San Antonio, Texas, and since of Stockton, California; they were all certified by Col. Adam Johnston, the Indian sub-agent referred to,[6] and yet at this day all the efforts of the parties interested have only reached the threshold of that throne of mercy but not of grace, the Court of Claims.[7] In these hours of national excitement

[4] Belt & Company were perhaps fairly honest, but some of the other contractors were not. In 1853 the reliable Edward Fitzgerald Beale, by then Superintendent of Indian Affairs in California, presented evidence that one of the three treaty-making commissioners had been involved in a dishonest contract for 2,500 head of cattle, and that one contractor had taken for himself a third to a half of the cattle due the Indians.

[5] A. G. Stakes (1818?–1873) came to California from Virginia by way of Texas and was one of Colonel Thomas Thorn's friends. He served one term as Judge of San Joaquin County. Even the *San Joaquin Republican*, while supporting his political opponent for the judgeship, conceded that Stakes was "a gentleman in every sense of the word."

[6] Johnston was appointed Sub-Indian Agent in April 1849; he arrived in California at the end of that year and was stationed in the San Joaquin Valley. He was a good agent, quarreling only with the men he should have quarreled with and giving real attention to the Indians until his disgust with the situation made him inefficient. Because of the plight of the Indians on their nearly sterile reservations, Johnston supplied them with more beef and flour than the treaties stipulated. His action in thus increasing the Indians' subsistence—as well as his arranging, without authority, for the vaccination of those under his care—received the complete approval of the acting Indian commissioner in Washington. But Congress did not appropriate money to pay the debts. Johnston was discharged early in 1852.

[7] The government refused to pay Belt & Company for all of the beef and flour delivered to the Indians under authority from Adam Johnston. By the time Sam Ward was writing this memoir, the claim for $7,826 had gone to trial, in 1855, and had been rejected by the Court of Claims, in 1859. Later the widow of George Belt renewed the petition. The case had ground along for twenty-seven years when the

and anxiety, arises the hope that if we are, like the *Great Eastern*, dismembered in a gale, to float asunder in two or more water-tight compartments, the new governments to arise out of this cataclysm may administer justice with an equity and meet their liabilities with a promptness to which the overgrown, chaotic and corrupt bureaucracy of our central administrations, by an unholy and tripartite alliance between Congress, the lobby and the departments, has long been a stranger.[8]

A few days were sufficient to familiarize me with the simple details of an enterprise in which hope was a much more considerable element than reality, and my attention became principally directed to the habits and customs of the Indian tribe, of which I was now the vicarious *paterfamilias*. I found it to consist of two clans—a larger, and the remnant of a smaller tribe. The chief of the former or greater Potoyensee[9] was Bau-tis-ta, who had received

court reversed itself in 1879 and finally allowed payment after hearing new evidence, part of which was a lengthy deposition by Sam Ward, and after being carefully reminded that Frémont had been paid, in a similar case, a quarter of a century earlier.

[8] It is a little surprising that Sam Ward, writing this in 1861, should attack the lobby. Although he is usually considered not to have become a lobbyist until after the Civil War, and although he certainly was not yet known as "King of the Lobby," he was active behind the Washington scenes as early as 1860. Milton S. Latham, Senator from California, kept a "Day Journal," in which he described several intimate Washington social-political gatherings involving Sam Ward, the earliest being on March 4, 1860. At one dinner that Sam Ward gave in 1860, Latham, Senator Gwinn, and Baron Rothschild were guests. Latham said it was a "party evidently for a purpose," and added in a footnote: "Purpose! Desirous of 'hiveing'!!"

[9] As with most California Indians, the name of these appeared in many forms, ranging through Potoyanti, Poto-yan-to, Poto-yau-tee, Po-to-yun-te, Poto-ancies, Po-toy-en-tre. They were sometimes referred to as Keeches, from the name of their chief. Frederick W. Hodge lists them as "probably Moquelumnan, formerly living about

a semi-Christian education in his youth at one of the Jesuit Missions,[10] where he had learnt to speak Mexican—respect to the Madrid Academy forbids me to call it Spanish—with tolerable fluency. He had also imbibed, in the sagacious school of the reverend fathers, not a few of the vices which are the thorns upon the rose bushes of their celestial gardens. With a passion for cards, a greater belief in the efficacy of a fleet horse, fine saddle, gaudy *sarape*, and a tall glazed sombrero with a silver band than of prayers to the saints or the Virgin, he had acquired great skill in the use of the lasso, having been the *vaquero* or cattle catcher of the pious institution to which he was attached. His manners were polished, and he wore a civilized air over the quiet dignity of the savage; his face was handsome, the expression of the mouth good-natured, but he had the fugacious eye of a London "cracksman" surveying a crowd, or of a gentleman on a Mississippi steamer playing poker "with the advantages." His form was athletic, with indications of better feeding, as well as breeding, than the rest of his tribe. . . . .[11]

---

headwaters of the Tuolumne, Merced, and Mariposa" rivers. At the end of January 1852, Adam Johnston estimated that they and the other tribe living in the *rancheria* at Belt's store numbered five hundred; by 1857, because of the influx of whites and the failure of the government to meet its promises, the larger tribe was said by an agent to have shrunk to eighty and to have been forced to some extent into "peddling their women" to subsist.

[10] Franciscans, not Jesuits, operated the upper California Missions in Bautista's time. Bautista had been attached to Dolores Mission.

[11] Bautista, Bautiste, or Baptiste was this chief's "Mission name"; his Indian name was variously spelled Keeche, Ke-chee, and Cechee. In March 1851 the commissioners who were to treat with the California Indians reported that after "waiting several days, the chiefs Tiposey and Bautiste (both hostile), with portions of their respective tribes, came in" and agreed to go into the Merced River Reservation. Wozencraft, one of the commissioners, later commended Bautista

The chief of the other tribe, old Trypoxi,[12] was a being of a higher order, though unadorned by those social and Christian graces which stamped his compeer a *caballero*. He was more dusky in hue (the other being of a bright and florid copper color) and spare of flesh, with a meekness and humility of manner which almost deepened into chronic melancholy. No episode of Mission flesh pots and scarlet kerchief had interrupted with enervating influences the sad monotony of his life struggle to keep together the small remnant of his once powerful tribe. The advent of the whites, and the comforts which they bartered for gold, had passed over his existence like sunshine over the sorrows it cannot dispel. I became subsequently greatly attached to this rare representative of savage self respect, honesty, and sensitive good faith; nor do I remember a more striking proof that the great Creator has planted all the elements of moral grandeur in the natural and unredeemed man. The intercourse between the two chiefs was as friendly and unassuming as that of the police captains of two contiguous districts in a well regulated city.

for his shrewdness, and told of taking him to Stockton and San Francisco in March 1851, to impress him with the power of the whites. Wozencraft said that the chief's father had been "tied up and executed" by a United States Army patrol in 1848 and as he died had "told his son to revenge his death." Wozencraft went on to express the unsupported opinion that "this led to the Mariposa war." The *Stockton Times* of March 26, 1851, reported: "The Indian Chief, Bautiste (Ke-chee) . . . . one of the first who made an open declaration of war to [Major] Savage, arrived in this city on Friday, in company with Dr. Wozencraft. . . . . He is about five feet six inches in height, is of stout proportions, and is reputed to be a chief of great courage and influence."

[12] When this chief signed the treaty of March 1851, he was identified as Trai-pax-e. His name appeared elsewhere as Typoxi, Tipose, and Tiposey, in addition to Sam Ward's spelling. His tribe sometimes was identified by various forms of his name, but it was more properly called Si-yan-te, Segante, or Se-an-tre.

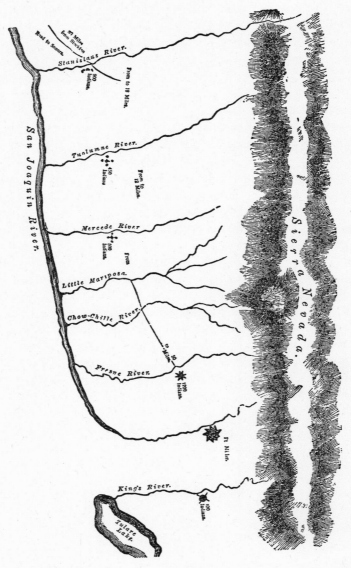

Agent Johnston's map of Indian reservations, January 30, 1852

58

A month may have elapsed after my permanent anchorage at the ferry, when one forenoon there were symptoms of great agitation in the Indian camp. Unintelligible words flew like arrows through the air, and the men and women left the river and hastened up the road in the rear of the store, which, at right angles with the Quartzburg trail, led to the Fresno, some fifty miles distant. I was at a loss to account for all this flurry among the apathetic Potoyensees, until informed that it portended the approach of Major Savage, the great Indian trader of the lower country, and even then was puzzled to know why his advent should produce a Prince of Wales' sensation. Dignity, of course, forbade my advancing to meet an unknown stranger, however distinguished, but, keeping my eye in the direction which the Indians were following, it was not long before I descried a cavalcade of some half-score trappers in appearance, slowly descending the bluff. As they approached the ferry, it was easy to detect their leader, whose yellow hair hung profusely below his shoulders, and who had something of that air-Napoleon which the habit of command is apt to impress upon those who wield it. His staff consisted of mountain men, who were the support of his forest throne; and I recollect that Judge Marvin, afterward Superintendent of Public Instruction in the Golden State, rode at his right.[13] The white Sachem dismounted, and entered the store with his

[13] The text spelled this name "Mervin" but referred to John G. Marvin (1815–1857), who was Superintendent of Public Instruction in California from 1851 to 1853 and was well acquainted with Major Savage.

Marvin apparently had considerable influence with the Indians, for in 1850 when they began actively to resent the mistreatment they were getting from the whites, a San Francisco newspaper thought him a good man to station among them.

suite.[14] I observed that his face was clean-shaved and his complexion sallow despite exposure in the open air, two traits quite rare among the bearded and bronzed population of the mines. It may appear singular that in stature, air, and feature, he bore a marked resemblance to the effigies I have seen of Peter the Great.[15] The Indians, particularly the women and children, thronged the store and pressed in crowds on the outside with all the avidity of the mob which struggles to enter an apothecary's shop into which a wounded man or a fainting lady has just been carried.[16]

[14] About sixty years after Sam Ward set down this reminiscence, William J. Howard, by then more than ninety, told his biographer that, as he remembered it, Kit Carson, Sam Ward, Adam Johnston, and he were in Belt's store on the Merced when the three United States commissioners who had come to California to treat with the Indians entered the store accompanied by Major Savage, whom they introduced.

[15] A newspaper of 1851 said: "Major Savage is a small but sinewy man, and probably does not weigh over 138 lbs. He has regular features, round face, light blue eyes, and his long yellow hair hangs down in ringlets like a young girl's."

[16] There seems always to have been controversy over the integrity of Major Savage's relationship with the Indians. There is evidence that he was by no means always honest with them or fair, but most of the California Indians seem to have regarded him with much the same interest and respect that Sam Ward's tribe showed here. At his death in 1852, according to a letter sent to a San Francisco paper, "the Indians threw themselves upon his body, uttering the most terrific cries, bathing their hands and faces in his blood, and even stooping and drinking it as it gushed from his wounds. It was with difficulty his remains could be interred. The chiefs clung to his body, and swore they would die with their father." A letter by the same writer, sent four months earlier to a Stockton paper from "Head Waters of the San Joaquin," suggested some of the reasons for the Indians' attachment to Savage: "Major Savage has just come over with a large number of Indians, and has given new life to everything in the neighborhood. He brought his wagons, ploughs, seeds, provisions &c.; and the quantity of work he has gone through with in a few days has astonished everybody. . . . . He has proved that these tribes may be taught agriculture and civilization as

With the Dowager Princesses of the Potoyensees he carried on a lively conversation, and his remarks were listened to with breathless interest, and at times elicited explosive delight. He was bound for San Francisco in search of some innocent assignee of his confidence in the solvency and the good faith of our Indian Bureau. Meeting with such an one, his design was to convert into cash his drafts and certificates of supplies, with a view to provide loads for his teams, which were shortly to follow him as far as Stockton. Our intercourse upon that occasion was brief and reserved, and his conference with the aborigines unintelligible to any of the whites present.

After his departure, this singular personage was the theme of conversation and comment, from which I learned that he had been the companion of Indians since his boyhood, having commenced his experience of their romantic life on the other side of the mountains, and was by some persons supposed to have a streak of their blood in his veins, an absurdity flatly contradicted by his hair, which was as fair as the golden locks of Achilles. I am unable to say how long it was since he had transferred his affections from the tawny lords of the eastern plains to their humbler prototypes on the Pacific slopes, but think I am correct in my recollection that he was one of the earliest emigrants thither, possibly, before the discovery of gold.[17]

effectively as any on this continent. The Indians all love him, to all appearance, and still he manages them in such a manner that they also fear him as much."

[17] James Savage when very young left home to live with the Sac and the Fox. In 1846 he crossed to California and in the middle of October joined Frémont's Battalion, in which he became the friend of two influential Indians with whom he went to live in the San Joaquin Valley after the Battalion disbanded. With the discovery of gold he went to the Southern Mines, employed Indians as miners, and soon established Indian trading stations on the Tuolumne and the Merced. By

He exercised over the tribes with whom he was in contact a magnetic and almost mysterious influence. His habits and nature were externally consonant with his name. He excelled the Indians in every athletic exercise and skillful accomplishment, and was their equal in his powers of abstinence and endurance, being competent to subsist upon roots and seeds and to perform those long dog trot journeys on foot for which that race is celebrated. I was told that, in his mountain home, he was as much of a polygamist as the meagreness of the Circassian market would allow,[18] and it was added that he often indulged on the Fresno in the luxury of native buff, with only the hiatus of a clout; a delicate piece of flattery to which Indian vanity was not unsusceptible.

This episode had flashed a new light upon my hitherto misty perceptions of Indian character. They were, it appeared, alive to other and deeper emotions than the superficial enjoyments of clothing and finery and the internal felicity of gratified appetites. The first step to their confidence was a knowledge of their language, which I felt an increasing desire to acquire when I listened to the wonder and admiration with which my messmates commented upon that Mezzofantine[19] feature in Major Savage's accomplishments.

My plans were soon formed to approach, if not to rival,

1850 he had built stations on the Mariposa and the Fresno, still far in advance of settlement. In August 1852, when he was about twenty-nine years old, he was killed in a quarrel that had its start in his resentment of a senseless slaughter of Indian women and children on Kings River.

[18] Much attention has been given Savage's squaws, their number being variously estimated from two to seven. These wives increased his influence with their tribes.

[19] Giuseppe Mezzofanti (1774–1849) was said to have spoken more than fifty languages.

the white Savage in this particular influence over the red.[20]
My relations with Bau-tis-ta had softened from polite reserve into growing cordiality. He spoke tolerable Spanish,
and would thus serve me as the black stone of Rosetta
did Champollion. So I invited his Highness to breakfast
on the following morning, and after having made him
too much of a Bologna sausage to feel inclined for the
rough work of river washing, got him into my sanctum,
placed before him a bundle of cigaritos, a tumbler of claret
sangaree and, with pencil and note-book in hand, asked
him to repeat to me the Potoyensee numerals. Not having
Mr. Ellis'[21] phonetic alphabet at hand, I contrived a sys-
tem of my own to express, now with Greek, now with
German, and occasionally with Latin characters, the vocal
value of such sounds as were foreign to our own language.
From the numerals I proceeded to the human family
. . . . and thence to human anatomy; next, to the wants
of man . . . . next, the cardinal points; then their measures of time—yesterday, to-day, to-morrow, etc.[22]

[20] Sam Ward was unlikely to rival him in one regard: it was said
that Savage had learned, to their awe, a secret language known only
to the major chiefs. How he learned it, if it existed and if he did, was
never explained.

[21] Alexander John Ellis (1814–1890), English phonetician.

[22] In a letter from the "Mercedes Indian Reservation," February
7, 1852, Sam Ward told his sister, Julia Ward Howe, that he had
made a grammar and a vocabulary of Bautista's language. These do
not seem to be among his papers today, but in that 1852 letter he recorded the following, here quoted verbatim.

Potoyensee—Regular Verbs

Inf.	Túyé-co-mi	to sleep	Inf.	Naté-mi	to know
Ind.	Túyé-ma	I sleep	Ind.	Naté-ma	I know
	Tuye-se	thou sleepest		Nate-se	thou knowest
	Tuye-co	he sleeps		Ne-te-ko	He knows
	Tuyé-co-ti	We sleep		Na-te-ti	We know
	Tuyé-no-ma	Ye sleep		Na-tey-noma	Ye know
	Tuyi-na-poo	they sleep		Nat-hen-po	They know

These lessons were continued as soon as I was able to digest their predecessors; in a few days I was trying my new wings in the air of the *ranchería*, exciting with my note-book the surprise and often the laughter of the crones and children who staid at home to keep the dogs from devouring the family stores.

The Nation, however, seemed flattered by this tribute to the beauties of their vernacular, and often when I was stalled for a word half a score would crowd around with eager good nature to help me out of the mire. In my walks, the urchins would follow me and impress upon my attention the names of flowers, pebbles, grasses, squirrels, birds, etc., that we encountered; so that I resembled Élie de Beaumont in one of those delightful excursions he used to make with his class, botanizing and geologizing in the environs of Paris,[23] save that, in my case, the instructions were imparted by my pupils. It was not merely to rival the Fresno trader in their *savage* affections that I undertook and accomplished the task of acquiring this new tongue; it was in itself a wholesome and entertaining species of mental gymnastics, excellent practice for mind and memory, neither of which can become utterly dissipated so long as their forces are centered even upon the humblest pursuit. . . . . Moreover, I had at times entertained the idea, if successful in acquiring the languages of that region, of making it my future business to possess myself, so far as practicable, with the other Indian tongues of the state, and contemplated with a certain glow of prospective pride the honor which might hereafter be paid to me as the "Old Mortality" of a race which seemed already reduced to the limits of their own graveyards. . . . .

[23] Élie de Beaumont (1798–1875) became professor of geology at the Collège de France in 1832.

California Indians catching grasshoppers for food

AMONG the various branches of industry contemplated by my friend's associate[1] in this scheme to render "The Ferry" the site, if not of a flourishing trading or manufacturing city, [of] a town which should vie with Quartzburg and Mariposa, was the manufacture of saddles. For this purpose, he had pressed into his service an ancient and well-seasoned Mexican, who professed experience in the composition of saddle-trees. Upon what precise terms this worthy had been engaged to contribute to the productive resources of the establishment, I have forgotten, if, indeed, I ever knew. Don Ignacio was a man of sixty whose wrinkles would not have disgraced an octogenarian but whose six feet of fleshless anatomy would have required but little preparation to fit them for a surgical cabinet. Where he had first drawn breath, he knew not, and his remembrance of younger and happier days was usually fainter than a dream. Mexican revolutions had tossed him from town to town and from province to province like a whirlwind which had gradually worked its way to the northward. To him all places were alike. A small bundle, tied up in a red handkerchief, contained his household gods; viz., his tools, a spare shirt, and a

[1] George Belt's name appeared in the title of the company Drought had bought into, and he was frequently considered the most important of the partners. But Drought's main relationship was with George Belt's brother, Upton, and it is almost certainly Upton, rather than George, whom Ward here called "my friend's associate" and farther on called "my principal's co-proprietor."

crucifix. Without a friend or a blood relation, he was the type of a human waif floating upon the surface of life, ready to cook, to saddle a horse, or to make saddles, and even to spin yarns for his food and lodging. Indeed, in the latter calling, he sometimes displayed vivid flights of imagination when he found an attentive listener; and would then indulge in graceful pictures, at one time of the estate of which he had been bereaved by treachery and ingratitude, and at another of his *hacienda*, stocked with fat cattle, etc., before it was pillaged and laid waste by an Indian raid. His workshop and tools were, if possible, more simple than those of an itinerant tinker—a knife and a hatchet with a hammer back sufficed for his manufactory. . . . . The saddle-tree consisted, in California as in Mexico, of four pieces—a loggerhead, two side plates and a crupper. This style of saddle even pervades Texas, where, as in the Golden State, the work of certain masters is more highly prized than the goblets of Benvenuto Cellini. Their great merit consists in their adaptation to the back of any horse without causing soreness on a long journey through extensive tracts of country, where grooms, stables, brushes and currycombs are unknown.

The two rivals in public estimation, in those days, were Hope of Texas and Graham of Santa Clara, whose naked trees would command from one to three ounces, either of which, it must be acknowledged, is a "fancy price."[2] By *naked* I mean covered simply with the thin, raw hide which holds the component parts together. Don Ignacio, like the sculptor in his studio, had one of these models before him, which he promised to surpass in grace and utility. A large order was sent to San Francisco for Mexican leathers to clothe their nakedness, and under the

[2] As Ward noted elsewhere in these reminiscences, an ounce of gold was then worth $16.50.

shadow of an oak on the river bank, the old man plied his calling from morn till night, with the persevering and concentrated energy of an unwearied cobbler; so that the store was soon decked with as many skeletons as the closet of Bluebeard. Although in a country where every man was more or less of a centaur the saddle industry might be supposed to have proved lucrative, I am not aware of its having brought any grist to our mill, for, whether our artist was untrue to his model or chose to indulge in deviations to suit his own fancy, it was impossible with every appliance and thickness of underlying blanket to make a ride of fifty miles upon one of his trees without rendering a horse almost unfit for future use. . . . .

In those days, the great Tulare valley abounded in mustangs, whose numbers were estimated at from twenty to forty thousand, and our Indians made frequent excursions in pursuit of them, and sometimes returned with a dozen or more, captured by the lasso. From the results of these expeditions, we often made purchases at from ten to twenty dollars a head for our *cavallada*, and these new acquisitions were "broken in" after the "*un*-Rarey" fashion of whip and spur[3] by a *vaquero* named Jose, who looked after our horses and cattle. He . . . . understood his business, never hesitated to mount the fiercest mustang, and was never unhorsed.

He was a *compadre* of Don Ignacio, and about three months after my settlement at "The Ferry" the two decamped for the southern country without leave or license, and when last seen had got beyond Pacheco's Pass. Their mode of exit inspired misgivings as to the amount of property they had taken with them, but no effort was made to overtake them, such episodes being frequent in the new country. Our stock of cattle and horses, though not large,

[3] J. S. Rarey (1827–1866) wrote *The Modern Art of Taming Wild Horses*, which stressed gentleness.

required to be "coralled" every night, and a Potoyensee
Indian, a brute of great pretensions and small performance, was selected as Jose's successor. So long as his duties
were confined to the pasturing of our herds, matters went
on smoothly enough; but one day amongst the lot of mustangs brought to us by the Indians from the Tulare a
large and powerful roan mare caught the fancy of one
of our proprietors, and the Indian *vaquero* was ordered
to break her. Such scenes have been too often described
to need a sketch at my hands. Since the Mexican War
and the acquisition of California, hundreds of thousands
of our countrymen have become familiar with the wild
start, the sidewise bound, the rear, the plunge, and the
stiff jump of the terrified horse endeavoring to get rid
of saddle and rider.

In the present case, the roan mare proved too much
for the professional cavalier; suffering him to mount her
three times, and after short but violent struggles stupe-
fying him with as many most intense falls, so that he
refused, after the third *fiasco*, to come again to "time." I
reproached Bau-tis-ta with this ignominious defeat of the
rough rider of his tribe, and invited him to take the animal
in hand himself. He declined undergoing the shock for
any sum short of a doubloon, but sent a lad to the
rancheria for his half brother, Sacate, who, he thought,
might undertake it for less money, having parted with
his horses and beads a few nights previous in a gambling
frolic at the Fresno. Unaware of the family relations of
his Highness, I had never before seen or heard of this
uterine brother, who bore a marked resemblance to the
Chief. Sacate came, and his poverty consented to break
the mare for two silver dollars. I had advanced to meet
him, and struck the bargain before he had time to receive
any more extravagant suggestions from his brother or
his comrades. He examined the mare with the eye of an

expert; ordered the saddle and bridle to be removed; made a noose of a hide thong, and passed the loop around her nether jaw to serve as a bridle; tied a strip of rawhide, hardly an inch wide, around the body; disencumbered himself of every thing save his clout; mounted her; thrust his knees under the ribbon of hide which encompassed her; grasped his improvised bridle; ordered them to remove the blind from her eyes and let her go.

The contest was exciting and charming. The bare legs of the Indian clung to the mare with the sinuous tenacity of an anaconda, while his body swayed to and fro with perfect ease and grace, anticipating her every saltatory spasm, and apparently as undisturbed as a child upon a rocking horse.

After having exhausted the most diabolical ingenuity without unseating him, she started off on a full run, and scoured the plain, making a dash of nearly two miles around it in what seemed to my eye a slashing pace, even for a thoroughbred. He brought her in panting, humble, and as subdued as one of Mr. Rarey's meekest specimens, and that without the use of violence. When he came for his money, he suggested an extra gratuity, alleging that every muscle in his body was still aching from the intense struggle.

It is not to be denied that the display of pluck addresses itself to the liveliest sympathies of our nature, and arouses emotions which no other human characteristic calls in play. It was this sentiment . . . . which last summer filled the hotels at Niagara with tens of thousands, admiring the audacity of Blondin and anticipating the slip of his stilts which might terminate his career in the abyss beneath.[4] Nor could I restrain my enthusiastic admiration for Sacate, whom I subsequently singled out as the object

[4] In 1860, for the third time, Charles Blondin, French tightrope walker, crossed the Niagara River.

of distinguished honor upon an occasion, the mention of which will now carry me some months ahead of my narrative.

It must have been in March, 1852, that I had occasion to visit San Francisco. The heavy rains of the winter season had nearly subsided, but the roads were still comparatively impassable, and I resolved to perform the journey after the fashion of the country with a *cavallada* of spare animals, and the Potoyensee centaur as my master of horse. I had been stalled once or twice in my peregrinations with white companions, who (with the exception of Mr. Lippincott, ever ready to dismount and assist a friend out of the mire) had left me to shift for myself; and I must confess to a pusillanimous horror of those *quick muds*, in which a horse or a mule flounders with desperation until he refuses to stir unless the rider lightens his burthen by dismounting. . . . .

Sacate gladly acceded to my offer of a peep at civilization—he had never left his native hills, and I anticipated from his survey of Stockton, the steamer *Sophie*, and the bay, harbor and town of San Francisco, all that reflected delight which one experiences in taking a boy to witness his first play. I rigged him out, regardless of taste or expense, in the loudest *sarape* and *calzoneros* the store afforded, and although our cavalcade consisted of but three beasts, besides those we rode, and two of them were mules, it was with a certain emotion of grandeur that I set out upon this journey.

We had not proceeded a mile beyond the river before I had cause to rejoice in the sagacity of my equerry, whose practical eye selected the most solid line of road and eluded many a tempting and treacherous mire. In the rainy season, green turf and smooth bits of road are to be avoided. Like a well-trained pointer hunting with a high nose, or a scout pursuing with the instinct of a water-fowl a faint and almost effaced trail over the grass of the prairie, Sacate shot on as if steering by compass, often dashing through the midst of small lakes in which the inexperienced wayfarer would have dreaded a watery grave. We thus accomplished stage after stage without interruption or casualty, and the led animals readily obeyed the every motion of the Indian, who seemed to possess over them the ascendancy of fascination. It was on the afternoon of the second day that we reached Stockton, in just sufficient season before the departure of the *Sophie* to quarter our animals at the "Tattersall's" of that town.

It now became my turn to act the pilot and to guide my bewildered savage though the streets in which it was almost impossible to get him away from the shop windows and to prevent him from pausing at every step to drink in, with staring eyes around and behind him, the panorama of this new world. It was a great relief to get him safely on board the steamer. . . . . After we had made a few miles progress and his amazement had softened into curiosity, I took my henchman down below to show him the engine, and entered upon the perplexing task of explaining the theory of steam and some of the intricacies of the machinery.

The Potoyensee language, it may be imagined, possessed but a moderate scientific vocabulary; in fact, I do not think it embraced a word corresponding to any portion of the engine. . . . . In my dilemma, I bethought me of the cook's galley, where, as supper was being prepared, I should have an opportunity of illustrating the motive power which impelled our vessel, by the effects of steam upon the lids of the saucepans in which our future food was stewing. Thither I accordingly led my pupil, and felt as proud of the inspiration as Pythagoras [*sic*] when he exclaimed "Eureka!" The sable chief of the pots and kettles entered cheerfully into my scheme of indoctrinating

71

the savage, and covered a pan with a tightly fitting lid, which the steam soon lifted; I was proceeding with my explanation, when a new and unexpected difficulty arose. We had ridden thirty miles before embarking, and the odor of the flesh-pots awakened other emotions than curiosity in the savage breast. Absorbed in my educational experiment, I could not think of sticking at trifles, and begged the cook to throw a "sop to Cerberus." The voracity of Sacate filled the Soyer and his dusky staff with inexpressible delight. . . . .

When we came on deck, the night was dark, though starry, and he stationed himself near the wheel-house, contemplating with silent wonder the phosphorescent, hissing foam of our cleavage through the black water; for we had emerged from the "slue" into the open bay, and the reader will acknowledge that the scene was calculated to inspire with a certain awe a child of nature whose experience of water had been confined to the streams and creeks of a mountain region. It was difficult to wean him from this new spectacle, and near midnight before I could prevail upon him to "turn in," in a stateroom where he paid his homage to the *genius loci* by stripping, like the votary at the threshold of the temple of Bacchus.

We reached San Francisco by daybreak, and Sacate, when he put his foot upon the wharf, surveyed the steamer with indications of greater satisfaction than he had exhibited when dismounting from the mustang. I little dreamed, however, the extent of his delight, or the depths of his previous apprehension; for it is a characteristic of most savage races to conceal their intensest emotions beneath the mask of dignified indifference.

There was already a lively show of palatial brick and mortar in San Francisco, which had just then arisen, phoenix-like, from the ashes of its second great conflagration.

Its tall warehouses of that color which pleases Indians and maddens bulls seemed to fill my companion with speechless admiration. I led him through the jolly streets to a small cottage on the hill, where I purposed depositing my blankets, and introduced him into the bed chamber of its distinguished proprietor, Judge M.[5] A subdued light came through the half-closed and curtained windows, and it was not without terror that my friend, suddenly aroused from slumber, saw the wild Indian in his rainbowed *sarape*, standing by his bed-side. My presence explained the apparition. Light was let into the room as well as the brain of the recumbent jurist, and a dialogue ensued, in which I acted the part of dragoman, of which I only recollect the concluding phrases:

JUDGE (*A fine looking man*)—Ask him what he thinks of me?

SACATE—I never saw such magnificent blankets!

I made several other early visits to friends in the vicinity, and about 9 o'clock proceeded with one of them, Sacate close at our heels, to the La Fayette Restaurant, the Delmonico's of the day. Recommending the Indian to the care of the maître d'hôtel, with instructions to supply him with as much as he could eat, and to "make a note of it," we sat down to a *dejeuner*, of which the omelet, cutlets, Chablis wine, &c., formed a delightful and touching contrast to our rude fare at the Ferry. . . . . when we arose the savage had disappeared, after consuming a dozen mutton chops, half as many beefsteaks, and [filling] up the interstices with various appeals to a round of bœuf à la mode and the bread basket. As our temporary residence was not far off, I presumed that he had repaired thither to rest from his dietetic labors, and proceeded to make

[5] Possibly Sam Ward's uncle, Judge Hall McAllister, Sr.

various calls in the business part of the city, without giving his eclipse a second thought. It was early in the afternoon when, returning to the cottage, I learnt with dismay that he had not returned thither, and, upon causing inquiry to be made by the police throughout the city, that he had not been seen by any one after his leaving the restaurant. A placard was immediately printed and posted conspicuously through the town, which conveyed, on pale sea green paper, the pleasing intelligence that one hundred dollars would be paid for the recovery of the missing savage, of whose appearance and costume a minute description was appended.

I remained in town ten days or more without any tidings of the fugitive.[6]

[6] On March 16, 1852, the San Francisco *Daily Alta California* began to carry the advertisement reproduced here as an illustration. It ran for several days. The *Daily Herald* carried a similar plea for information.

uilding,
ancisco.
K.
1mc

N—Wash-
begs leave
pened the
ie" bread,
t and eggs,

will please
ieir wants,
ar13 7*c

Proprietor
announce
celebrated
situated a
d the Pre-
comforta-

r13-1mh

.—BAR-
r the Tea-

Lost and Found.

LOST—An Indian accompanied by a gentleman from Mariposa, arrived in this city on Sunday last, and has been missing for the last twenty-four hours. Being an entire stranger and ignorant of our language, it is feared that some casualty may have befallen him of which he has been unable to apprize his friend. Any information as to his whereabouts, left at the office of the Alta California, will be thankfully received. He was dressed in a blue jacket, brown striped pants, woolen shirt, green drab hat with black binding, and was without shoes. mar16

BROUGHT TO THE ECLIPSE LIVERY STABLES, Dupont street, a black horse branded on the near thigh and shoulder, which the owner can recover by proving property and paying charges. If not called for within ten days he will be sold at public auction to pay expenses J. M. McDONALD,
mar16-3*c Per W. H. RAWLING.

DOG LOST—TEN DOLLARS REWARD. Strayed from the Subscriber, on the 12th February, 1852, a small Terrier Pup, about three months old, buckskin color. His ears and tail were not clipped when he vamosed

On
with
On
suite.
Ap
feb

tifully

may

neat
sion a
mar

two e
mar

T
The

THE *Sophie* touched the Stockton wharf at break of day, and my first care was to repair to the stable where I had left my *cavallada*, which I found as lusty as feed and rest could make them. Having directed that they should be got in readiness for the road, I took my solitary breakfast with intrinsic misgivings of the discomforts awaiting my homeward journey. To ride my best nag and worry along the other four over a fenceless highway would be unalluring to a centaur, and was anything but soothing to the fancy of a moderately good horseman, whose ambition and strivings had been hitherto limited to the performance of equestrian solos, with the occasional variation of a lost stirrup or a tumble. Fortunately the rains had desisted during my absence, and the roads were said to have improved. Coffee and reflection brought no other relief to my dilemma. It was indiscreet to look up a volunteer *aid de camp*. A stranger might prove a "Tartar" and take French leave with my animals or venture upon greater extremities, like Mr. Ruxton's Mexican equerry who, riding behind his master, drew a deliberate "bead" on him over a horse-pistol on the morning of their second day's journey together. The ball passed through the knight-errant's hat and spared the head to which we owe one of the most charming narratives in the English language.[1] Nor did the appalling reckoning of hay and barley charged

---

[1] In his *Adventures in Mexico and the Rocky Mountains* (London, 1847), George F. Ruxton described this misadventure, which took place between Durango and Chihuahua.

to my quadrupeds admit the idea of incurring the further expense of hiring a palfrenier. In those days, every article of food for man and beast was sold in California by the pound—it was all weight and no measure. Think of weighing such ponderous things as potatoes! The general price of barley in the mines was from twenty to twenty-five cents a pound, and in other regions as much less as the cost of transportation. I remember once passing three days in Grass Valley, where my hotel bill was twelve dollars and the stable reckoning of my horse, twenty dollars! . . . .

One of the ostlers had an errand to French Camp, a few miles beyond Stockton, and very materially aided me in extricating my cavalcade from the streets of the town and the entanglements of occurrent teams. He was one of those impulsively benevolent creatures who catch runaway steeds in crowded cities and are the first to . . . . jump in after a drowning man . . . . When fairly on the road, he so far counteracted, with whip and shout, the dispersive proclivities of my little drove that before we reached French Camp they had fallen into line. . . . .

I reached the Stanislaus late in the afternoon, without accident. The ferry and the hotel were then the property of a Mr. Heath, who added to the comforts of a well kept inn the grace of good breeding and the welcome of hospitality.[2] In driving my animals, I had incurred as much more fatigue than from an ordinary journey as the pointer dog does beyond the sportsman who follows him. An elk had been shot by the Indians the day previous, and, would I stop to supper and breakfast, he (Heath, not the

[2] Heath and Emory, as partners, took possession of Taylor's Ferry in 1850 and built, at the close of that year, a pontoon bridge over the Stanislaus which the *Stockton Times* believed to be "the first in California." The *Times* went on to say that the operators of Heath & Emory's Ferry had "done more to improve the Stanislaus road than any other men."

76

elk), would send on my spare animals in charge of a friendly teamster, who was expected from Stockton at sundown.

These temptations were not to be withstood, particularly as the grass afforded excellent cropping in the clearing, and I should only need barley for the chestnut *macho*, on which I intended pushing home on the morrow. The Ferry House had more than pretensions to cottage elegance —a broad and well-roofed verandah flanked two of its sides; a natural lawn sloped down to the river, beyond which, and on all sides, the eye rested upon copses and timber. In those days, there was no [other] such *caravanserai* in the Golden State.

Did you never withhold a question of the deepest interest to yourself, for fear of an unsatisfactory or disheartening reply? I confess to that weakness, and I often refrain from asking the paying teller "whether that note has been put to my credit?" and when I meet my broker, after a fall of stocks, I dread to inquire whether he realized mine before the decline. . . . .

I was once reading the newspapers in the *Lonja* of the city of Mexico, where my *palace broker* had left me while he went to the cabinet meeting at which a transaction in which I had a heavy stake was to be approved or rejected by President Santa Anna. Immersed in a lot of fresh journals, received by that day's *correo*, I looked up when Senor M—— returned after an hour's absence, and then continued my reading. He sat down opposite to me, and followed my example. We had been thus engaged for at least half an hour, when he arose and suggested a walk. As we closed the door, I observed:

"Well! I suppose that proposition went through?"

"Not by a great deal—we are postponed to the Greek calend."[3]

[3] Meaning that the request would never be dealt with.

77

How I rallied and won on the following day may be told hereafter.[4] In the present instance, I was dying to ask Heath whether Sacate had passed his ferry, and could not at first frame the query with composure. I had just resolved to inquire, with an air of indifference, what day my Indian went up, when mine host, suddenly remembering my triumphal passage down a fortnight before, asked abruptly, "What on earth have you done with your Indian?" . . . .

When I told him my story, Heath shook his head, and suggested sending a messenger to the Merced, to inquire whether the fugitive had been heard of, before I ventured back. This was repugnant to my instincts of rectitude, and I declined. Few calamities had ever found me so entirely in the right, and I resolved to indulge in the unusual luxury of a stainless conscience and meet the issue. The matter was freely discussed at the "euchre table" that evening, and an old mountain man gave me a gleam of comfort by the assurance "that where there were watercourses, an Indian was always sure to find his way home."

I made an early start on the morrow, and took Mr. Heath's parting words as the text of my ambling soliloquy: "If that Indian has not been heard of at your camp, and should not make his appearance in double-quick time, I recommend you a change of climate."

I rolled up the twenty miles or more between the Stanislaus and Dickenson's[5] ferry on the Tuolumne in

---

[4] Although Sam Ward was probably in Mexico more than once, this anecdote perhaps came from the trip he made in 1854 to negotiate with Santa Anna for the release of the prisoners taken in the defeat of Count Raousset-Boulbon's filibustering expedition.

[5] The name of the owner of this ferry appeared in various forms in Sam Ward's text and in the newspapers of the time. But he seems to have been Gallant Duncan Dickenson, who was born on the Atlantic seaboard, settled in Tennessee, had moved by 1832 to Missouri, and in

season for a leisurely bait for myself and mule. I desired the option of speed or lounging, as I had yet to elect whether to reach home in broad daylight or after nightfall. When I learned from my landlord that he had no tidings of the runaway, I decided to adopt the former alternative, and got underweigh shortly after noon. I was not without hopes of finding Sacate at the *ranche*, and, if they shared my ignorance of his fate, the sooner the country was scoured the better. In this frame of mind I approached the bluffs of the Merced towards sundown. I had rode the twenty-two miles in a trifle less than four hours, which was quick work over the still boggy road.

Talleyrand divided mankind into two classes—the friends and the enemies of baked apples—but one of my most valued friends resolved men into "those who played hammer and those who played anvil." This time I was determined to "play hammer," and to hold his kith and friends responsible for the trick Sacate had played me. Had not his disappearance detained me in San Francisco a week beyond my intention, and occasioned anxiety and expense, to say nothing of disappointment? For I had promised myself much pleasure in the psychological study of the effects of civilization upon so thorough a child of nature.

My appearance upon the bluff speedily brought the boat across the river; and as I had left my other animals behind, they who saw me alone upon the *macho* presumed

1846 arrived with his family at Sutter's Fort in advance of the snow which engulfed the Donners, with whom he is said to have traveled earlier. After a period in the mines, where a gulch near Mokelumne Hill was named for him, he settled at Stockton in 1849, built the first fair-sized hotel there, and served as prefect of the San Joaquin District. When his Stockton property burned, he bought for $12,000 the ferry on the Tuolumne that appeared as Horr's Ferry on early maps.

that my equerry must be bringing up the rear with the remainder of the *cavallada*. The Indians were in the river washing for gold, and upon reaching the store, I retired to my room and dispatched a messenger for Bau-tis-ta. His Highness obeyed the summons with alacrity, and could not suppress his astonishment at his brother's eclipse, although he manifested no alarm nor even uneasiness at the circumstance. The lad, he said, was always a shy and wild creature, whom the missionaries had failed to catch when they brought him, Bau-tis-ta, into the fold. The big city and crowds of people had frightened him, and was I sure he had not been kidnapped and carried to sea, he would answer for his way back to the *rancheria* by land.

He left me abruptly to tell the story to his people before ill-nature, ignorance, or suspicion should have time to distort the facts and produce an impression unfavorable to me. After allowing what seemed time enough for the chief to perform his mission, I strolled into the store to be overwhelmed with questions, to which I replied with patient minuteness, endeavoring with some success to give a semihumorous turn to the incident, though professing all the while such indignation as I had a right to feel at the unceremonious proceedings of my companion. Bau-tis-ta and his family acted as my *claqueurs* with a chorus of grunts and applause whenever the enthusiasm or faith of my audience seemed to flag. There happened to be a patch of bare and smooth earth around a tree, to which the teamsters' horses were usually tied when taking barley. On this improvised blackboard I drew a chart of the country to Stockton, and tracing our road down, I represented Sacate and myself by a couple of acorns and our nags by pebbles—a carpenter's chip answered for the ferryboats of both rivers. I drew a rough outline of Stockton—put a burning cigarito upon a larger chip to denote the *Sophie*, and illustrated, with the contents of a cup of water artistically poured upon the ground, the greater water (*oyani ricken*) through which she ploughed her way to San Francisco. Leading them through the city, which I could only describe as a monster *rancheria* of houses in comparison with which our frame store was no bigger than the cooking stove inside of it, I wound up by a description of their comrade's Polyphemic assault upon the larder of the La Fayette Restaurant. At the recital of this last exploit, sympathy (to use the expression of my old shooting companion, the late Billy Bottimore, of Newport)[6] "started the gastric" and my hearers adjourned *en masse* to the shambles . . . . clamorous for beef . . . . The two chiefs, Bau-tis-ta and Trypoxi, did me the honor of supping with me, and after vainly essaying to emulate the performance ascribed to Sacate, old Trypoxi observed that the lad must have been laying in, on that occasion, a supply of food for a long journey.

For the ensuing three days, two or more of Bau-tis-ta's kinsmen, or lieutenants, were continually hanging around the door of my sanctum; and when I sallied forth for my "constitutional," I had a body guard of volunteers, besides sundry urchins who seemed beating up the plain or the woods before me, as if engaged in a battue or a German *treibjagd.* One night, when I had been reading "Bleak House" until a late hour, I opened my door and found one of the chief's half-brothers stretched before it, and as I was closing my window, an Indian awoke beneath it and bade me good-night.

The dignity of my position forbade any inquiry into the motives of these unusual attentions. Were they pre-

---

[6] The text spelled this name "Bottsmore," but referred to Bottimore, a quaint character in Newport who took Sam Ward and his brothers hunting and fishing in the eighteen-thirties.

cautions against my escape? or were they anticipatory of some peril to me? I withheld these speculations from the whites attached to the *ranche* for, upon the slightest intimation or rumor of danger to me being put into circulation at Quartzburg or among the miners up the river, lots of Texan rangers, "spoiling for a fight," would be down with offers of the friendly service of extermination.

I think it was on the third evening after my return that, shortly after dusk, I heard the "death wail" cleaving the air of the *ranchería*. To my inquiry, "who had died?" my attendants replied that some of the crones of the village, in despair at Sacate's continued absence, had given him up as dead and were indulging in the "luxury of woe." I dispatched a message for Bau-tis-ta, whom I reproached with this scepticism, and invited him to accompany me to the huts and aid me to remonstrate against these needless lamentations. He recommended my letting them cry it out, adding that he had grown hoarse in deprecating the suspicions which had culminated in this display of grief. That during his education at the Missions, to which he had been carried a child and lured by the eye and the palate (raiment and food) into forgetfulness of his mountain origin, his tribe had fled to the hills, and brought up Sacate in their savage persuasion; that his influence was that of birth and rank, without the ties and sympathies of association, etc.

His objections did not deter me from my purpose of visiting the camp to reason or reproach the mourners into tranquility. He begged me to put caps on my revolver, and gave some orders in a low tone to a couple of his pages, who stealthily took divergent routes for the *ranchería*. I marched down alone with Bau-tis-ta, having bidden him dismiss those of late my usual escort.

I was resolved to "face the music," and did so with a serenity to which the honesty of my conscience, in respect

A *ranchería*

of the absentee, imparted a sort of moonlight repose. Several tents were vying in lugubrious threnodies, performed by the gentler sex. . . . . As I entered, successively, these abodes of mourning, I waved my hand to command silence, and then upbraided them with their little faith in me, who had been their father and benefactor for so many months —who had never broken a promise, nor deceived them in the faintest assurance; that, had evil befallen him they were needlessly deploring, and had I been the author of his mishap, I were a madman or an idiot to come back amidst their tribe. . . . .

Then Bau-tis-ta addressed them in his fashion: "You are fools and noodles to lament one whom I, his brother, and all the rest of his family, feel sure is alive and safe, and will return. It is a reflection upon our good sense and our affection that you should pretend to be wiser than us, and display grief for which we see no cause."

The poor creatures listened to our appeals with the humility of unresenting sorrow; one or two replied, in a kind of Runic stanza: "We are few upon earth, and soon shall be none; our brother is not here, and we weep; if he returns, we shall rejoice."

All the annoyance, or rather impatience, which had inspired my errand, could not resist melting into sympathy with sorrow so heartfelt and submission so mournful. I returned saddened to my room, and soon heard the irrepressible dirge of the desponding resume its ascendancy over the stillness of the night.

On the following morning, I received letters from San Francisco, which apprised me that the police had traced my fugitive to Prospect Hill, in the rear of the city, where he had been seen hovering in the *chaparral* at about noon on the day of his disappearance. These advices also mentioned that he had left his *sarape* behind him in a corner of the house from which we had taken our departure for that memorable breakfast.

I made these facts known to Bau-tis-ta, who argued, from his abandonment of the *sarape*, that his brother had started for home after having rid himself of all encumbrances. His only possible *sortie* from the peninsula of San Francisco was to follow the shores of the inner bay, and at its extremity—San Jose—strike for Pacheco's Pass and the San Joaquin River, to which our little stream was a tributary. The utmost distance, by this round-about course, would not exceed two hundred miles. It was a fortnight since his disappearance, and a week was more than sufficient for so untiring a pedestrian to have accomplished this journey: "Provided," added he, "the poor boy have not come to grief in supplying himself with some one's else horse on the way!!"

Upon this supposition, we laid our plans to dispatch a brace of scouts to the San Joaquin on the morrow, with a

84

passport from me to serve as far as Pacheco's Pass, while I would write down to my friends to have inquiries instituted, and a reward offered in San Jose and its vicinity. We had hardly digested this project when the clamors of loud voices drew me to the door of the house, where I witnessed and participated in the singular scene, which, after the fashion of romance, I shall defer until the ensuing chapter.

THE PRINCELY family of Potoyensee, like its European prototypes, consisted of an elder and a younger branch. During Bau-tis-ta's long seclusion (I will not call it captivity) in the Jesuit[1] Missions, the duties of chief or rather regent had devolved upon the most prominent member of the latter. The name of this Duke of Orleans was Feliz, whom, from his predatory habits, I always suspected of having stolen the small Spanish vocabulary he possessed.[2] Upon the advent of our countrymen as previously mentioned, legitimacy prevailed, and Bau-tis-ta, released by the dismemberment of the Missions from his detention as a hostage for the good behavior of his tribe, resumed his sovereignty. Had the advantages of this dominion been embellished by a "civil list," the regent would probably have become a usurper. But as the chieftancy involved no other perceptible privilege, besides its honor, than that of being spokesman of the tribe, it was said that Feliz retired with becoming grace from his temporary throne. Bau-tis-ta was eminently popular with his lieges, whilst Feliz, though so many years the "bell wether" of the flock, seemed to have inspired few attachments. . . . .

Since my sojourn at the ferry, Feliz had not been a

[1] Franciscan.

[2] Feliz was one of the eight headmen who, with Bautista as chief, signed the treaty of 1851 which put their tribe on the reservation at the Merced.

86

constant dweller at the *rancheria*, though his handsome wife never attended him upon his frequent excursions, now after mustangs, now after antelopes, and sometimes after the accumulations of the Indians on the Fresno. He was a restless, uncontrollable spirit, insensible to the amenities of life, unless in view of some material result. . . . . He excelled in the chase, and usually hunted alone.

It was he who had brought up Sacate during the eclipse of Bau-tis-ta, and a warm attachment between them was the consequence. For a horse dealer, Sacate was a valuable ally, and had probably acquired, from association with Feliz, those Bohemian proclivities which the reader will shortly see developed.

But to my narrative. When I went to the door I was warned back to my room by two of my volunteer body guard, who said, "Don't go out! Feliz is there drunk and wicked." It was no time to yield to apprehensions. Extremes of heat and cold blister the skin alike, and a big and menacing peril which has not yet ramified in the imagination may at times seem a broad and risible joke. I returned to my room, adjusted a freshly loaded navy revolver, and emerged from the house.

Feliz, on horseback, in the midst of a crowd, who seemed endeavoring to divert if not to restrain him from some purpose, was flourishing a horse-pistol and vociferating in a voice trembling with passion. As if I had been the game he was awaiting, my appearance drew upon me with concentrated energy a torrent of invectives and menaces, enforced by disagreeable demonstrations of the pistol, which I saw at a glance was not cocked. The Indians pressed around the horse, and with clamor and remonstrance sought to urge him away. I ordered silence, and asked the infuriated savage the meaning of this disturbance and the cause of his grievance. His reply was nearly in the following words:

87

"I came back last night to my people, and found my brother Sacate was gone. Our women mourned him for dead; you took him away, and have either slain or sold him. Life for life, and I want yours."

Suiting the action to the word, he discharged his pistol, which he had cunningly cocked unperceived. As he fired, a tall cousin of Bau-tis-ta who stood upon the other side of him caught him by the arm and pulled him towards him, which raised his aim, and the ball entered the house some three feet or more above my head. It was a very fair *line* shot. All eyes were fixed upon me. My "navy" was levelled in a second upon my treacherous assailant. His life was in my hands. A frontier man would have taken it on the spot, but I held him at the end of the pistol for some moments, and then said, "You deserve death for that shot; death for having attempted to kill the bene-factor of your tribe. If the white men up the river knew this, they would make bloody work with you all. I neither sold nor killed your brother Sacate; he ran away from me and will return; if not, others have detained him and he alone is to blame. You are drunk and crazy, and I spare you for the sake of your tribe." Turning to the Indians, I commanded them to bind him hand and foot, and put a guard over him until morning, when I would pass sentence upon him.

Infinitely relieved of the anxiety which the well-known retaliatory habits of the white had inspired, the Indians sprang upon him and *did him up* like a bale of goods or a *papoose*, and hustled him away to his tent. I remained in the doorway until the crowd dispersed, when the women of the tribe drew near with grateful faces, and contended for the honor of kissing the hand which had spared a brother. . . . .

Shortly after dark, Bau-tis-ta and Trypoxi paid me a visit with some little ceremony, the object of which, I soon saw from their studious avoidance of any allusion to the afternoon's "scene," was to ascertain my intentions with regard to the principal actor. We had resumed our discussion of the best mode of ascertaining the fate of Sacate, when a cry like that of some strange bird or animal interrupted our dialogues. We listened, and the sound was repeated. Both exclaimed, with a simultaneous yell of joy, "Sacate, Sacate!" The emotion of the two chiefs was infectious, and crept over me like gooseflesh. In a few moments Bau-tis-ta had sufficiently recovered his composure to tell me that, for the purpose of recognition at a distance in the dark, every one of his tribe adopted, from childhood, a distinctive cry or scream; that the sound we had just heard was Sacate's howl, passed on, as it were, by telegraph, perhaps two or more miles from the camp. It was his howl, but not his voice, and sure enough, a tap on the window in a short time called our attention to the bloodless face of a panting Indian boy, who announced to his chief that his royal brother was approaching with a *cavallada* of strange horses. This revelation seemed to convey a world of meaning to my visitors, and to explain the predatory temptations which had lured the fugitive from what Dante calls the *diritta via* "out of the woods."

It must have been a full half-hour before the scapegrace made his appearance . . . . meagre as a skeleton, and almost naked. His first exclamation was "food!" and in a few moments he had dispatched all the economies of our meat-safe, and was grinding hard biscuit with a ferocity which I should have been glad to transfer to our quartz stampers at the Washington vein. I had, meanwhile, mixed for him a large tumblerful of claret sangaree, and when he looked up for a drink, I insisted upon his answering my first question, "Why did you run away?"

"I was afraid of the fireboat and the big water."

By this time, the hum of many voices told us that the

89

ranchería had poured forth its inmates, who thronged the outside of the house, all joy and curiosity. I ordered Sacate to go to the door and proclaim to the crowd that he had left me of his own accord, through fear, and not from unkind treatment. The intelligence was imparted in a trice, and they dispersed, exclaiming *"po-to-lok!"* (the Potoyensee for astonishment). . . . .

Sacate's narrative was eagerly listened to. He had no sooner touched the wharf at San Francisco than he re-solved not to return upon the "tea-kettle." In the rear of the city he saw hills and *chaparral*, to which, after breakfast, he quietly repaired. Lying *perdu* in the bushes during the day, he formed his plans of escape from the dilemma of steam and "big water." At nightfall, he prowled among the paddocks and cottages about the town in search of a horse. He found one tethered in an en-closure which, from his description, I argued must have adjoined the residence of Capt. Folsom, U.S.A., who was then lying ill with the disease which has since deprived the Quartermaster's department of an efficient officer, and San Francisco of a public spirited citizen.[3] The color of this *borrowed* steed happening to be white, he lost no time in exchanging him for a darker animal out of the first *corral* he encountered on his way to San Jose, on which occasion, two horses being like two heads—better than one —he borrowed another, and riding all night with the speed of John Gilpin, and stopping to relay at every new *corral*, he found himself by daybreak in the red woods back of New Almaden, with four steeds requiring a day's rest. In this way, journeying only by night—for he had a thievish fear of daylight and white men—sometimes losing himself in his preference for thicket and timber over the beaten path or the smooth plain, he had reached Pa-

---

[3] Captain Joseph L. Folsom (1817–1855).

checo's Pass, subsisting entirely upon the remembrance of "that breakfast," and such roots, herbs, and seeds as are found in the floral of Indian woodcraft. A gipsy, under similar circumstances, would have entrapped the poultry as well as the quadrupeds of the dwellers by the wayside, but Sacate's notions of appropriativeness were confined to the nobler animal. By the time he reached the Pass, his cavalcade consisted of eight horses, the *élite* of the valley of San Jose. At Pacheco's, becoming somewhat embold-ened by success, he made his first *jornada* by daylight, and encountered but one wayfarer—a Mexican *caballero* in the same free and easy line of business as himself, with whom he made sundry exchanges, as the *raid* of the former had embraced a diametrically opposite line of country. This trade lessened Sacate's stock by two animals, which were represented in his "balance sheet" by saddle, bridle, and spurs. He had swum his drove across the San Joaquin River the day previous, and hoped to reach the Fresno in the morning, as, upon inspection, some of the brands upon the animals showed them to have been the property of parties very apt to enforce the possessive pronoun.

I was no magistrate, and the whole adventure of an Indian rolling down the other side of Prospect Hill, and all the way to Pacheco's Pass, with the acquisitiveness of an avalanche, was so pleasing a contradiction of the detest-able adage, "a rolling stone gathers no moss," that I could not divest the performance of that "ridiculous" which is separated only by lath and plaster from the "sublime." If it be true, according to La Rochefoucauld, that we take a certain sly pleasure in the misfortunes of our friends, was it to be expected that I should feel sorrow for those of such entire strangers as had contributed to swell the cavalry of the dexterous Indian?

Here endeth the episode of Sacate, which I have fol-lowed out in anticipation of my narrative, in pursuance of the new historical method adopted by the late Mr. Prescott, in his "Life of Philip II," in which the siege of Rhodes and the battle of Lepanto are introduced as great historical frescoes, above the altar at which Thalia is chanting the anthem of Escurial life.

On the morrow, I ordered Bau-tis-ta to summon to his tent Trypoxi and the dignitaries of both tribes, to take cognizance of my decision *in re* Feliz, against whom I pronounced sentence of banishment from the Merced region, with the penalty of being shot or hanged if found within a radius of ten miles of the *ranche*. I descanted upon the enormity of an offence which might have occasioned almost the extermination of his tribe. I compared their condition to that of their brethren in other parts of California, who were so frequently sufferers by the injustice and cruelty of the whites. Here they were allowed the uninterrupted prosecution of river washings insufficient to tempt the greed of my people but quite rich enough, with moderate labor, to supply their more modest wants. The return of Sacate, whose disappearance had subjected me to odious imputations which culminated in the mad attempt for which Feliz was about to be punished and of which the injustice had been proved by his return, afforded me the opportunity for a moderate flourish of self-laudatory trumpets, and I had the satisfaction, at the close of my address, of perceiving that the sentence and "charge" were received with unqualified approval. The two chiefs were instructed to communicate his doom to the criminal, and to see that its provisions were enforced. Half an hour sufficed for the poor devil's preparations. A mule carried away his wife and child—and a horse, himself and the remainder of his worldly possessions. When I saw the outlines of the sad couple on the horizon, above the hill over which the path led to Major Savage's camp, I felt sincere sadness at having been compelled to inflict even so

92

moderate a penalty upon so humble an enemy; but I steeled my heart with the reflection that, according to the criminal law of civilized society, I had but condemned the individual to suffer for the good of the many.

Consistence with "Prescott's law" justifies me in adding that Feliz, on his way to the Fresno, was engaged by some inn-keepers, named Howard Bros.,[4] to purvey game for their establishment, to which he was still attached as deer-stalker two or more years after my departure from the Ferry. I met him on one occasion— a flying trip to Frémont's *ranche*—on Lost Creek, when he approached me with the cordiality due to an impartial judge from a magnanimous foe.

[4] These were the two Howards who were associated with the Belts. In conversation with his biographer in the 1920's, William J. Howard recalled that in the gold rush to Mokelumne Hill he had been saved from mistreatment at the hands of the miners by a chief whose name in the biography is spelled "Falis." Howard went on to say that the same Indian later worked for him.

FROM THE episodical escapade of Sacate, I return
to the jog-trot of my narrative, which I left when the
Indian centaur appeared upon the scene and interrupted
the tranquil seclusion of idyllic life.

The reader has already been put in possession of the
simple elements which composed the establishment of the
Ferry. . . . . Let us leave the Alban villa for imperial
Rome, the banks of the Merced for Quartzburg, where
science and machinery were about to develop the hidden
wealth of the great Washington vein.

When the last wagon of the procession, which had been
straggling across our ferry laden with weighty packages
addressed to "T. C. Flournoy, Treasurer,"[1] had had time
to reach its destination, I mounted my *macho* one fine
morning, and arrived at Col. Thorn's by breakfast time.
A meeting of our company had been summoned for
the following day, and pursuant to American custom, it
behoved me, as the representative of the various friends
whose proxies I held, to anticipate by a little preliminary
canvassing the measures to be adopted by our united wis-
dom on the morrow. It had been whispered that I might

[1] The text gave "B" as this man's middle initial, but official
quartz records called him Thomas C. Flournoy. As early as December
15, 1850, he recorded discovery of a vein near Quartzburg. He was
associated in several others with such men as Thomas Thorn and
Joseph Tivy, and in one claim he was a partner with Sam Ward. In
May 1852 he was listed as one of the seven trustees of the Washington
Mining Company.

be offered the post of superintendent, an honor and a responsibility of which I was not ambitious, for I had sought retreat in quest of repose, and as a majority of the directors resided in the neighborhood I felt appalled by the idea of carrying on works in which I was a novice under the eager eyes of interested critics. . . . .

Such did not appear to be the opinion of Mr. G——, a spare and pale New Englander who had made his appearance there with encomiastic letters from two of our San Francisco stockholders and was an anxious candidate for the honor for which I felt no inclination. He had (as what Yankee has not?) a tolerable knowledge of machinery, running gear and the steam engine.[2] The mass of mankind is led by such thin and restless spirits of the Anglo-Saxon race to whom trouble seems none. They are skippers of fishing smacks, and commanders of Indiamen, schoolmasters and preachers, overseers and cotton factors; the first in a railroad accident to suggest the readiest mode of replacing the overturned cars upon the track, and in a steamboat explosion, to preside over and draw up the resolutions of a meeting of the survivors, censuring the owners, who are five hundred miles away, and the captain, whom the disaster has thrown much farther. . . . . Mr. G—— drank milk, and did not play cards, which passive virtues lent a gilt edge to his volume of miscellaneous experience and acquirements. He accordingly received the unanimous vote of our meeting, and entered at once upon his functions

---

[2] The possibility is very good that this was E. B. Goddard, who on October 20, 1851, with several men known to have been interested then in the Washington mine, claimed a vein immediately adjacent to the Washington. Goddard, if he was the Yankee mechanic Ward referred to, kept up his interest in machinery; for in 1859 the *Alta California* reported that the employees of the Pacific Foundry in San Francisco gave a present to E. B. Goddard, one of the proprietors, as he left for a visit with "his friends and family in the East."

A crude stamp mill

with a salary of five hundred dollars per month. The services of a competent engineer who had been detained several days by the expectation of our necessities were secured at three hundred dollars per month, and a lead miner from Wisconsin, who had had some experience in magnified gunpowder blasts during our Mexican War, completed our mining and engineering staff. . . . .

To extract [gold] from the rebellious rock, in which nature had buried it with a view to stimulate the courage of labor and the genius of invention, was no ignoble undertaking. Instead of trusting to the blind goddess to reward hope with sudden and substantial realities, we had to place our reliance upon the endurance and capacity of our machinery, and upon the "chilled" stampers which were to crush the quartz with iron tyranny. New problems continually arose in the inception of quartz grinding. To be sure, in Wales, Cornwall, and even Virginia, such appliances had long been in use for the pulverization of ores, but the rock in Californian ledges was far tougher, and much rougher in its wear and tear upon iron and steel, than any mineral to which stampers had hitherto been applied. The problem to which I allude was one of labor-saving, viz.—by what process to reduce the greatest possible quantity of auriferous rock, in a given time, to impalpable powder? This may, at first sight, strike the reader as a question of easy mechanical contrivance, and so it is, upon a small scale; but when one comes to the trituration of tons of rock in a day, containing, by analysis, some three cents of gold to the pound of quartz, and one needs to grind five or ten such tons to pay expenses, the problem assumes proportions incommensurate with the result of minute experiment. Supposing the rock of easy extraction, and the vein of tolerably regular yield, and that the masses ejected by every "blast" are susceptible of ready clearage by the hammer which breaks them into fragments about twice the size of the component parts of a McAdam turnpike; when the mill is fed with these morsels of fortune, which are kept "under the hammer" until pounded to a powder sufficiently fine to pass through the minute wiregauze screen, whence they escape in a stream of water into the amalgamating tubs beneath, you have only conquered your first two difficulties. The process of amalgamation is by no means a spontaneous absorption of the fine particles of gold by the hungry quicksilver. Should the mercury chance to be greasy or otherwise unclean, it rejects, instead of taking up, the gold, and even when purified by constant use it is often capricious, preferring the precious metal in certain rocks, and discarding it in others. Thus, if they all contain sulphur, the mercury has greater affinity for the baser substance, and the gold flows away in the water current to enrich the "tailings" of the mill. In our case, we forced all the grindings through the quicksilver at the bottom of two rows of tubs, one placed beneath the other, and the heating of the stream of water by the steam of the engine added thirty per cent. to the yield of the mill. Every quartz mill has at least twelve stampers, which are successively lifted and dropped by spokes arranged spirally upon a revolving cylinder, not unlike the teeth upon the barrel of a huge hand-organ, adjusted for a chromatic scale.

The weight of our stampers was one hundred and twenty-five pounds each. In other mills, they were as heavy as five hundred pounds, and when I left the mines the most appropriate weight was still unascertained. This was eight years ago, and though numberless improvements have since been made in machinery and processes, I have yet to learn of success having attended operations upon a great scale and moderately rich ores, by which I mean those exhibiting from two to five cents per pound. At least one-half the gold then escaped in "the tailing"; it may be less today. Where quartz mills have succeeded and must continue to prosper even with poorer ores is in cases of the association of mechanics and miners, who pay only the ordinary wages of labor and earn and pocket their own salaries. . . . .

I HAVE SEEN quite a number of autograph letters of the First Napoleon; the best of them resembled in their chirography the trail of a spider rescued from an inkstand by some member of the Humane Society and suffered to crawl over the paper. These were penned in calmer moments. There were others, written in the saddle, which might be styled *hieroglyphics in cypher* were such an alphabet imaginable.

My last number was indited not in the saddle but in an earthquake. Amidst the convulsive throes of the day preceding the Inauguration of President Lincoln, on the Fourth itself, and the day following, the immature cry of the printer's devil for copy haunted me like the "still small voice of conscience," and my response to the invocation was as vague and impatient as your answer to the inquiring urchin at your side in the fifth act of a new tragedy.

I think it was the late Gouverneur Morris who, celebrating the restoration of the Bourbons in a discourse from one of our city pulpits half a century ago, dashed *in medias res* with the exordium: " 'Tis done!—the long agony is over, and France reposes once more in the bosom of her legitimate King!" There is a reduced parallel in the event of the 4th of March, '61. The agony was a short one— but Abraham Lincoln has been inaugurated, although he came near realizing that famous "slip 'twixt the cup and the lip" with which experience has made us all more or less familiar. He is our "legitimate king" for the next four years, and yet there are many who hope that his reign will smack more of Cromwell than of Louis XVIII. M. Blondin carried a man on stilts across the Niagara chasm; but Mr. Lincoln has to sustain a nation on his shoulders with more turbulent waters foaming at the bottom of a deeper abyss.

. . . . On the Isthmus of Panama, before the railroad, there were, in the mule days of 1849–52, one or two . . . . gashes in the rock so deep and narrow that two wayfarers could not pass one another. To avoid such encounters, a shout was raised at the entrance, and if answered by no echo from the other end, the enquiring cavalcade was safe to enter.

Presidents Lincoln and Davis now appear at either extremity of such a pass. . . . . A voice was heard some weeks ago from the Montgomery end of the pass, and on the fourth of March the answering echo was trumpeted from the Washington extremity—Heaven avert a collision![1]

Before the curtain shall rise upon the third act of this National Drama, let me lead the reader back to the River of Grace, in which I may be excused for wishing the extremists of both parties, the Yanceys and Slidells, as well as the Greeleys and Phillips, might be either drowned or re-baptized!

It was late in the autumn [1851], just after winter's first premonitory showers, that I saddled my Frémont mule and rode up to Quartzburg one Saturday morning. On the Monday previous, a blast had uncovered the butt end of what promised to prove a streak of rotten quartz and oxidized iron scoria—so dear to the gold miner. When I

[1] Early in February 1861, delegates from six seceded states, meeting at Montgomery, Alabama, adopted a constitution. On March 4, 1861, Lincoln declared secession invalid.

reached the hamlet, I found Thorn Villa deserted, save
by the ladies of the family. The Colonel and his friends
had gone to the mill to see the result of the week's mining,
pounding, and amalgamation. I hastened thither. Its clat-
tering stampers were silent—the engine was cooling off—
the water had been let out of the amalgamating tubs, and
the superintendent was scooping into an iron pan the mercury graced with yellow promise. In a rude chamber ad-
joining, five or six stockholders and directors were await-

An improved stamp mill

ing the trial. I entered after Mr. G——, who deposited upon a bench before the Treasurer the first instalment of amalgam.

The reader is of course (or should be) aware that quicksilver can be squeezed through the pores of buckskin. Where it is charged with gold, the fluid escapes, leaving behind it the denser and more precious residuum. . . . . A "lap" is made of the buckskin by holding the four corners, as the muleteers grasped those of the blanket in which Sancho Panza was tossed. The loaded mercury is then poured in—the corners joined form a temporary sack, and the squeezing ensues.

Miners are generally satisfied when the residuum which refuses to pass through the "chamois" is no bigger than a hickory nut. An English walnut induces palpitations of the heart, and any larger mass brings on delirium. *Our first ball was the size of a pippin!* The next five showed no diminution—and even the mercury from the six lower tubs gave us as many filberts! What a dessert! . . . .

Composure was difficult under such circumstances. It is easier to compress the upper lip which grief strives to lift like the throttle valve of a steam engine than to prevent the rebellious corners of the mouth from dimpling into a smile. So we all went with more or less of a broad grin to the fire in the open air which was to sublimate in the iron retort the mercury which had captured the gold. This ungrateful process may seem like murdering the tame elephant which has just caught you a wild one—but the nozzle of the retort is immersed in water which re-captures the [mercury].

The retort is unscrewed—the golden fruits carefully removed, and the interstices of the honeycombs examined to calculate the richness of the residuum. The balls are then patted like Norman butter, and become quite solid in their cohesion. When "the little jokers" had likewise undergone the calcining process, the treasure was transferred to a linen bag, and we adjourned *en masse* to the store and to the gold scales upon its counter.

We had to weigh the lot by instalments, and the grand total was three hundred and sixteen ounces—equal to five thousand and sixty-four dollars, at sixteen and a half dollars per ounce!! If my memory serves me, we poured out a libation of "peach and honey" to Plutus, and then drank it ourselves. . . . .

Whilst the more jolly of us were interchanging felicitations, I overheard the superintendent inquire carelessly of Capt. Tivy, at what hour the stage passed down the next day. . . . . I felt that his object was to give early intelligence to his friends in San Francisco that they might profit by the information. He certainly had a motive for the question; and the only alternative conjecture was that he intended "vamosing" with the gold, which was highly improbable. Nay, his character from below and the evidences he had given of that shrewdness which forbears "cutting open the goose that lays the golden eggs" forbade the uncharitable supposition. One of my gunpowder trains took fire, and I made up my mind to anticipate the rise in Washington stock, if my animals could get me to Stockton a day before the stage.

So I saddled up Frémont, and, taking leave of the rejoiced associates, and particularly of the superintendent, I noticed a placid smile upon his grim visage when he saw me turn my mule's face towards Mariposa. Had I gone home, his imagination might have conjured up my phantom scouring the plains "express" to get ahead of his calculations. As I often paid Mr. Killaly a visit, to get news from the mysterious interior of Bear Mountain and pick up the last amalgamative contrivance, my departure in that direction excited no surprise.

Three miles beyond Quartzburg, I executed a wide

detour, rendered tedious by hills and *chaparral*, and returned to the *ranche* by an Indian trail I had noted on my frequent shooting excursions. I reached home an hour before dusk. The store was full of customers, for the Indians had had a field day—I invited Bau-tis-ta to share the meal prepared for me, and then proposed to his Highness to pay a visit to the Tuolumne Reservation, which, though under my general supervision, I had not yet inspected. This *rancheria* was on the river a few miles below Dickenson's Ferry, where I purposed passing the night so as to get an early start for Stockton the next morning. He gave some directions to a youngster—we took a quiet supper, and then lounged over the Ferry, where the lad held our nags and a horse to be led, which I reserved for the hard ride of to-morrow. We got away unperceived—it was soon dark, and, having a perfect right to change my mind, I did so, and after making four or five miles, we diverged and galloped over to Dickenson's. The chief was always glad of a change and accepted the gambit without a question. We reached the Tuolumne in season to be heard from the other side without needing artillery to wake up the inmates of the tavern. The ferry-boat came noiselessly over the dark water, like the ghostly canoe in the Arabian legend of the Prince in search of the Magic Mirror, which was to test the purity of the fair candidates for his heart and throne. We embarked and met with an unusually cordial welcome at the hostelry—mine host, a Missouri rifleman, had been shooting salmon in the afternoon "and was just wishing I might come along to enjoy a plenteous fish supper."

I arose an hour before daybreak, and pushed on to Heath & Emory's Ferry, on the Stanislaus, before breakfast. There my nag and I took a couple of hours of rest, always pleasant on the grass lawn for the quadruped and beneath the shelter of the verandah for his master. At 10

A.M. we resumed our journey, and got to Stockton a couple of hours before the *Sophie's* departure.

At Quartzburg, I was presumed all this time to have been "passing the rosy" and enjoying the legitimate consequences of that pleasing ceremony under Mr. Killaly's roof at Mount Ophir!

I was anxious to have an hour or two in Stockton, that I might fall in with several stockholders in "the Washington" who had been original proprietors and had paid up their assessments without having received any dividends. Although "black care sits behind the horseman," fortune is said to favor the enterprising. I had made a forced march of seventy-five miles since the evening previous, and the blind goddess rewarded the performance by prompting the very people I wished to meet to find themselves successively in the paths of my afternoon peregrinations. The result was that I became the proprietor of one hundred and fifty more shares at the price at which our party had been "let in" to the enlarged company. The next day I reached San Francisco at dawn, and went to the house of a military friend, who has recently signalized himself by his efficient preparations for the defence of Washington against the "surprise party" supposed to have been organized for its capture before the 4th March.[2] I made him my confidant, and resolved to lie *perdu* for a day or two. He succeeded in capturing about fifty shares held by outsiders, which was all that could be purchased without seeking to buy out our own friends, with whom loyalty forbade tampering.

The next morning, although the superintendent did not come in person, his letters must have reached his friends. There was an extraordinary curiosity among the members of a certain moneyed *clique* to know "who had

[2] Charles P. Stone, formerly an Army officer, served early in 1861 as Colonel of the District of Columbia Volunteers.

any Washington shares for sale." There was no reason assigned for the inquiry, which, perhaps, had its mysterious effect upon the imaginations of stockholders. The shares which we had taken at $14 rose at once to $35, and my friend, the Captain, disposed of my purchases at that figure, and refused to take more than 5 per cent commission, although I would have divided.[8] Others of our party sold enough of their shares to reduce the cost of the remainder to 0, and when all these little "averages" had been consummated, I made my appearance in town, and confirmed the encouraging reports which the new buyers had received from their friend the superintendent.

I thought this little operation not only lively but justifiable at the time. It gave me a "pocket full of rocks" for many a week, and appeared to please every one concerned. I am not proud of it to-day; though the parties of whom I bought were not my intimates and had I, with my usual good nature, whispered in their ears, "Hold on to your shares, they are a treasure," they would not have paid sixpence for the information. Had they been Wall Street Pirates, I should still twinkle my eye over the feat in moments of elation—but these sellers were "innocents"; what chance had they with one who had parted with half a million to buy his own experience? I therefore should now feel remorse for the achievement, were it not useless to cry over "spilt milk."

But I am wasting my regrets in the wrong quarter— it was, after all, only the hungry buyers who suffered.

The deposit in our tubs, that famous week, came from a "pocket" and not a vein! The kobold who performed the miracle of fortune, although *encored* until the thin superintendent became a skeleton and my purse an empty

[8] If Frank M. Anderson is correct in connecting Ward with "The Diary of a Public Man," Ward later may have repaid Stone's favor; for the "Public Man" commended Stone to President Lincoln in 1861.

mockery, never condescended to reappear before the stage lights! The vein was worked for eighteen months or more, and "just paid expenses."[4] Some of us consoled ourselves with the reflection "that we were lucky not to be embarrassed and sold out, like many of our contemporaries." Some enjoyments lose their zest and pall with their chronic continuance. This was my case. I had become as accustomed to declarations and protests as a Turk is to fleas, and derived no comfort from the above salutary consideration. Neither did I repine at the sterility of the mine.

This would have been ingratitude, for I had made a "good thing" of it, though the golden fleece of my argonautic journey had been torn by the thorns of circumstance and had gone the way of all—except kept—gold.

I have still in my possession my certificate of the shares which were kept to "take the chances"—it lies in an old tin box with a variety of engravings promising treasures in the Lake Superior copper region, in Texas and elsewhere which I hold at the service of any friend disposed to indulge in "Spanish Castles"—the only species of architecture in which such currency is freely taken in payment for labor.

---

[4] The *Mariposa Gazette* years later printed a letter from a correspondent at the Washington Mine who said that the "vein is quite large, but the pay rock has usually been found in bunches, generally separated by large bodies of slate, which have occasionally confused the miner and disheartened the owners."

But the chief sources of disappointment to the owners in the early years were poor stamp mills and high wages, which led Erasmus Keyes, one of the San Francisco partners, to write to Rodman Price in May 1852, after a visit to the Washington: ". . . . I found the mine good, but the expense of working it is too great. In the month of April last the amount of gold taken from the mine was upwards of $11,000! And still the mine is in debt $4,000, and between you and me, I do not think we shall get a dividend this year. . . . . I intend to sell as soon as I can get a good offer. . . . ."

THE FERRY at the *ranche* was already "in the full tide of successful experiment"[1] when my principal's co-proprietor came to pitch his tent and his fortunes upon the Merced River. He accordingly selected a spot nearly a mile higher up stream, at the base of the first rising of the Quartzburg road, where the river, one-third narrower than at our crossing, struggled plainward between two bluffs not less than twenty feet high. It was at a bend where the stream, emerging from the timber, "doubled" as if pursued by the shades of Actaeon's hounds. The water was deeper and stiller, and seemed to be gathering breath for its scamper over the rapids which impeded navigation between the two stations. The new location possessed advantages over its competitor which will shortly be made manifest. At low water the banks were unpleasantly steep, and loaded teams, unless clogged, rushed on to the boat with the rapidity of a sled down a *Montagne Russe*. The *ranche* had the advantage of a more gradual slope on the bluff bank of the river, and ascending wagons, once ferried over, had little or no grade to surmount on their way to our khan. Whether the advantage of being first on the trail gave the Howards a lion's share of the travel, or whether he thought poor company better than none, it is certain that not long after his settlement in the valley the co-proprietor effected a fusion of interests by

---

[1] This was one of the first ferries established in the San Joaquin Valley. It was originally called the California Ferry.

A California store

which one of the brothers[2] was transferred to the Tuolumne and the other[3] to a station some eight miles farther
south, on the road to the Fresno. . . . .

I must have resided nearly three months at the *ranche*
when, returning home one day from an excursion to
Quartzburg, I found no little consternation among our
assistants at the prospect of an opposition ferry being
opened at the bluff which the co-proprietor had abandoned
when he joined the Howards. There had been a "scene,"
and nearly a "row," between him and the squatter in question, a man named Wilson, who had formerly been a
ferryman in his employ. Although he had ceased working
the crossing, the co-proprietor still considered himself the
owner of the location, with which he further flattered
himself that no one would dare encroach, and finding his
menaces met with unexpected determination, he had gone

[2] William J. Howard.   [3] Thomas Howard.

to Mariposa to obtain from Judge Bondurant[4] an injunction, which seemed the more agreeable method of getting rid of the intruder.

To me, this was an unexpected phase of ferry life; I had never dreamed of such a contingency, and it was only when I heard this one and that one say: "I told him he ought not to let go his hold of that crossing—but he *would* bring away his shanty which served to keep possession of the spot, &c.," that I became acquainted with the legend of the two ferries, their fusion, &c.

I felt little uneasiness as to the new comers. Ours was an established post. Its business had been steadily improving, and were we to have this opposition we must meet and conquer it by superior management and increased attention to the wants of our customers. It was one of those blunders which Talleyrand stigmatizes as "worse than a crime" to have neglected the very simple precautions that would have prevented the intrusion. I could "wash my hands of it," though I found no bliss in the ignorance which had kept me hitherto unconscious of the danger.

While the co-proprietor was absent, the "army of occupation" slowly entrenched themselves in the position. A tent arose; a boat was launched, and one or more teams wound their way along the opposite bank with lumber and wares for the new store. This suggested some peril to the Indian traffic of ours, and I accordingly assembled the chiefs and heads of families and told them very plainly that if any member of a wigwam were found selling his gold dust or buying goods at the opposition shop, I should at once stop all supplies of beef and flour

[4] The text spelled this "Bongirand" but referred to James Bondurant, formerly of Alabama, who was judge of Mariposa County while Sam Ward lived there.

to the whole tribe. I was at that time distributing four beeves and eight sacks of flour a week—all of which, as I have elsewhere stated, still remain unpaid by the great Father at Washington.

This menace was sufficient to "taboo" our rivals and isolate them as completely as the Castle of Lochleven. The co-proprietor returned unsuccessful in his application for an injunction, but the *ranche* retained its travel and its Indian trade. Soon after it became evident that our custom was not likely to fall off, I strolled up one afternoon to the opposition *ranche* and made a *reconnaissance* of its improvements, in one of which they excelled us; this was the attraction of a rosy damsel behind the bar,[5] who proved to be the daughter of the principal proprietor—a grey-eyed Englishman named Phillips,[6] who bore a rotund resemblance in person, face, and even *strabismus* to the learned and ingenious Professor Mapes.[7] I broke the ice by ordering a bottle of porter—price one dollar—and wound up by extracting from the landlord the good-natured and candid avowal that the dullness of the locality was quite discouraging; few whites passed that way, and whenever he beckoned a loitering Indian to

[5] The *Stockton Journal* in 1852 said: "There are fewer of the fairer part of creation in Mariposa county than in any other part of the mines."

[6] John Phillips arrived at the mines in 1849, having come overland. He is said to have made a trip east in 1851 to bring his family to the Merced. Although he seems ultimately to have been successful with his ferry and store, about a year after he started the establishment he found it necessary—surely in part because of Sam Ward's taboo—to mortgage for $1,400 his half-interest in Phillips' Ferry and all of his right to an adjacent one hundred sixty acres on the south side of the Merced "with a large tent and frame house thereon."

[7] James J. Mapes (1806–1866) taught science at the National Academy of Design and organized the Franklin Institute at Newark, New Jersey.

the store, "the varmint would take to his heels like a strange dog."

I took a look at the ferry; its fastenings, ropes, &c., were new and convenient, but the steepness of the descent on either bank comforted me with the inference that nothing short of a deluge could render its competition formidable. After this inspection of "the elephant," I no longer felt a pang when an occasional team strayed away from our crossing. Several wagoners, who had tried it for the novelty of the thing, returned to us on their way down. "They liked our crossing best. Wilson was a surly ferryman, whilst our boys were always *piert* and obliging; old man Phillips was a decent body, and his daughter good to look at; but the cut was steep, and then we were always jolly, &c."

The days grew shorter. The rainy season was approaching and might come upon us at any moment "like a thief in the night." The store-keepers of Quartzburg and Mariposa were nearly through with hauling up their winter stock of goods and provisions. I had paid Mr. Killaly my last antepluvial visit to Bear Valley, and noticed that several intervening "dry creeks" were dyked on either margin by embankments of auriferous earth and sand, dug and hoarded in summer and autumn against the advent of the rain, which should convert the hopes of their patient and laborious proprietors into realities more or less golden. At the foot of Mount Ophir, Mr. Killaly had commenced his gold reductions with a series of colossal Mexican *arrastres*, near which lay hecatombs of ore, whence he anticipated fabulous results; his intention being to grind day and night for three months without stopping to make dividends—a process which, followed by the N.Y. Chemical Bank, resulted in quadrupling the value of its shares.

A gathering scowl in the heavens hastened my return

An improved *arrastre*, or Chile mill

home. It was near the end of October. In some years the Californian rains delay their appearance until Christmas. The sky thickened steadily for several days, and one or two preliminary showers seemed to be the "scrapings" of the Celestial Orchestra before initiating the winter symphony in earnest. Our ferry-boat was now tethered every night to the overhanging limb of a stout tree on the opposite bank—the usual precaution when we were threatened with a flood. A robust, five-inch cable held our ark by the nose (bull-fashion), and as the branch to which this hawser was fastened stretched out some ten feet above the water, the boat had rope enough to "veer and haul on" for a rise of twenty-five feet in our Nile.

Without prefatory thunder, the deluge came.[8] The rain fell in torrents for a day and a night, at the expiration of which the river had gained ten feet, and the ferry-boat was on a level with the branch it was tied to; there

[8] Stockton newspaper accounts reported that the Southern Mines had five days of heavy rain beginning on November 8, 1851.

was no abatement on the second day, and our Neckar had
become a Rhine, tearing by us with sullen impetuosity of
turgid and swollen flood. It was by this time one hundred
and fifty yards from edge to edge, and the current too
swift to venture over in the light canoe which was our
sole means of communication with the boat struggling
on the other side. Towards noon its ravages in the upper
forests were revealed by an endless descent of floating
logs, and these were soon followed by planks, cradles, and
other evidences that the freshet had invaded the mining
valleys above us. The opportunity of laying in a supply
of fire wood was too good to be neglected, and the bank
was strung for half a mile with Indians fishing for logs,
now with hooked poles and now with loaded cords, in all
the varieties of attitude observable on the rocks at Newport of a bass-day. The rain poured on and the flood
continued to gain; but much more slowly. All the lower
bottom lands on the river were overflowed, nearly doubling
the width of its channel. It was far above last year's high-
water mark. . . . .

The pleasing activity of the Indian portion of the
scene—the successful anglers hauling in wooden prizes,
and the urchins of the tribe rolling them high above the
reach of the torrent—was interrupted by a shout which
warned them that the back water was encroaching upon
their *rancheria*. In an instant leaving their piles of fuel,
the natives rushed to their menaced fire-sides, and in a
couple of hours, the Indian village had been removed to
the bluff in the rear of the store over which Maj. Savage
had made his appearance. A traveller approaching the
ranche on the Fresno road, while the Potoyensees were
anticipating May-day, might have imagined them Mac-
duff's soldiers transporting "Birnam Wood to Dunsinane."
Half an hour was quite enough for the reconstruction of
a hut. Some of the poor devils had caps of coarse sheeting

to spread over the apex of their conical thatches, which protected a small space from the rain-torrent—but in most of their wigwams there was no better shelter than would be afforded beneath a hemlock tree in an open grove.

Towards nightfall all eyes were centred upon the boat, which the rising stream had lifted several feet higher than the now submerged branch to which it was fastened. The river was gaining several inches an hour, at which rate our ark must either be submerged or break loose from her moorings at an early hour on the morrow. I stood in the doorway until pitch dark and watched her bravely holding her own, and before "turning in" I detected by an auscultation of the confused "voices of the night" what I fancied to be the flapping of her stern upon the uplifting waves after the fashion of the fluke of a harpooned whale.

The howling wind and the rain smashing upon my windows, and occasionally driven by a fiercer gust like a crash upon the weather-side of the house, interfered with sleep. In the "catnaps" stolen from the tumult without and my own anxieties within, I dreamed of being at sea— a vision to which verisimilitude was imparted by the reflection, in my waking moments, that a rise of eight feet more must bring the flood to the level of my floor. . . . .

The first gleam of dawn through the morning mists found me on the lookout for the boat, and I soon descried it, like a phantom Leviathan, high up in the branches of the tree from which it was struggling to escape. The freshet had gained four feet in the night, and although rising but about two or three inches an hour must invade the store by sunset. In one corner lay huddled a score or more of Indian women and children, who had availed themselves of the permission, extended to all whose household arrangements were incomplete, to enjoy a night's dry repose. I roused the cook, and had an *arroba* of *frijoles* set a-boiling. The news spreading that there was to be a soup-morning brought half the tribe to the store, and I made a liberal offer for volunteers to swim the river and carry a line to the boat, which must soon reach the end of its tether. The beans were handed over in large mining pans to the conscript fathers of the tribe, who dispensed them with an impartiality and enforced a freedom from clamor which would have done credit to the discipline of the mess captains of a man-of-war.[9] I have enjoyed few greater pleasures in my life than the happiness afforded to those comfortless and friendless numbers on that eventful morning. The cook was directed to renew the *pot au feu* until there should not remain an empty stomach in the tribe. I again looked forth. The rain ceased falling at about 9 o'clock, and the sun occasionally peeped between the white bars of clouds from a patch of "steadfast blue." But the sky was still black in the northeast, and the river still creeping upwards. The rain had not ceased in the mountains and the freshet was not yet over.

Warmed up by the unexpected breakfast, the Indians were clamorous that the two stoutest swimmers of the tribe should try to reach the boat, and once there pay out more rope to the branch which held it, or, failing to untie the knot, endeavor to fasten it to one of the upper limbs of its anchor-tree. The distance to be crossed was not two hundred yards, and one of the swimmers walked up the river a quarter of a mile or more until he reached a spot from which his eye judged that he could strike the boat. He made his plunge, and, gallantly buffeting up stream, seemed likely to attain his quarry; five hundred

[9] Sam Ward could speak of life on a man-of-war from experience; for several months during 1858–59 he had lived aboard the frigate *Sabine* on an expedition to Paraguay.

eyes watched the struggle from the river bank, and now and then a cheer would arise as he gained obliquely upon the other shore; then a yell of disappointment as he struck the deep channel which hugged the opposite bank! The swift, strong current turned him fairly over when he met it; but in a moment he rose and rallied against the torrent with desperate bravery; he was swiftly borne down towards the tree—three more strokes, and he must clutch its branches. He leaps out of water like a flying-fish; another effort and he is safe! He makes the spring and grasps the branch, and his body is swayed down length-wise by the stream. He tries to get an overhand hold, and to draw himself up to the tree; the *branch snaps*, and he is whirled swiftly past the boat, head under! But no! he did but dive like an otter. There is a bend in the river below; he makes for it, crosses successfully, and emerges dripping and disheartened a quarter of a mile down stream. Crowds rush to meet him; he shakes his head as he draws nigh; his pride is wounded by the failure. I tell him it was the tree's fault, not his. Coffee and biscuit renew his courage. He takes his comrade aside, and they consult with a tall and intelligent, but weakly, brother of Bautis-ta. They have formed a plan. They want fifty fathoms of clothes-line cord, a water-tight box, and my air pillow. The store furnishes the line—I splice it together—the raft is made. It floats high out of the slack water. They transport it about a hundred yards higher up stream than the last point of departure. Their plan is to swim to the boat with the raft between them. Each holds in his teeth a bit of wood, to which the boat-saving apparatus is fastened by a fish line about a yard long; they strip and are ready.

Each takes a swallow of whiskey toddy—galvanic stimulus for the supreme effort. They push off from the bank and breast the stream like Siamese Twins, with our ferry's life between them; they husband their strength for the ferocious current of the deep channel; they attack it like tigers clutching a boa constrictor; they are cutting it fiercely in two, and as they approach the line of river above the tree, we all see that they must strike plumb on the boat. Huzza! *Potolok!* They have grappled it, box and all! Their upstretched hands, clutching the bow on either side of the hawser, are lifting their bodies into the ark, when, oh, dismay! *the cable parts!* and boat, raft, and Indians are whirled down the torrent with the swiftness of a locomotive! The brave savages make a desperate effort to turn its head across the current—but at the bend it takes the downward sweep and floats away a wreck, while the swimmers, clinging to the raft, land a mile or more below the store.

The disaster was serious, but not irreparable. The Indians were rewarded. Their exciting struggle was a lesson of energetic philosophy, and I had the melancholy comfort of feeling that the co-proprietor, as he cast a glance towards Phillips' Ferry uninjured by the freshet, must have experienced pangs of bitterness in comparison with which my regrets were a joke.

Why had he not left a pawn there, to defend
his king's row upon the
River of Grace?

THE CATASTROPHE had occurred shortly before noon; and whether the wrath of the elements had been sufficiently appeased by the destruction of our ark, or the river deities compassionated our distress, the sky continued to "clear up," and the Merced began at once to fall. . . . .

Our Indian scouts returned in the afternoon with tidings of the boat, which had lodged upon an island little more than a mile below the ferry. It lay there like Shaw, the Guardsman, after the battle of Waterloo, upon a heap of slain,[1] and was the worthy apex of a hecatomb of prostrate trees, logs, and smaller fragments of timber. Postponing our visit to the scene until the next day, we spent the evening in consultation and conjecture. Some of us had hopes of a "reconstruction" of the wreck, but I had seen too much of the force of waves upon timber to imagine that a rude ferry-boat, subjected to the tension and battering of the freshet and then dashed high and dry by a ten-knot current, [could] be restored to life and buoyancy.

Fortune had favored us with a couple of guests, whose accidental delay at the *ranche* proved most opportune. One was a sturdy carpenter named Smith, the untiring zeal of whose plane and saw made amends for the impediment in his speech, which constituted him a better listener than

[1] According to legend, this corporal in the Second Life Guards cast aside his saber at Waterloo and killed many of the French barehanded before he himself was killed.

119

talker.² The other was a small, spare weasel of an Eastern man of forty, by profession a well-digger, in which capacity the co-proprietor had, on several occasions of financial abundance, employed him to delve for water near the house without success. Both were glad to offer their services on dull-season terms, and when our bargain had been concluded I felt that we were as far out of our difficulties as Mrs. Glasse was when she had "caught her hare."³

It seems singular now that the name of the well-digger should have been "Uncle Abe," and I trust our Washington *ranche* may yet be under the same obligations to his homonym as we incurred to the old proletarian whom Providence sent to our aid upon the River of Grace. He had once tended a ferry upon the Ohio, where a similar accident had occurred. Nay, with the exception of a stray "meeting-house" or school-house which once in a while gladdened the people near Ford's Bar, where he first learned to fish for wandering logs, the resemblance extended to every incident of ours. . . . . His counsel was to let the river drop for a day or two; meanwhile he had taken a stroll up stream in the afternoon and found a magnificent "canoe log" a quarter of a mile above Phillips' Ferry, and, foreseeing it might be useful, had cut his name upon it, which was good property law. By the time the river should have shrunk he and Smith would have a tip-top canoe ready, and then a boat-yard could be established wherever it suited us best. St. John Chrysostomus never let fall more golden words. Our worn-out skiff had been damaged, and was past caulking. A solid canoe would make us masters of the river, and I had hap-

---

² This carpenter presumably was the one named P. T. Smith who testified in 1879 that he "was in the employ of George G. Belt & Co. on the Merced River, from June, 1851, to January, 1852."

³ "First catch your hare" is said to have developed from one of the eighteenth-century recipes of Hannah Glasse.

pily a couple of gutter-adzes among the tools of the store.

Early in the morning we repaired to the waif. Wilson, the ferryman, was there before us with a manifest inclination to appropriate it. "Uncle Abe," in reply to his surly question about our right to it, showed him his "title" cut in the bark the day previous, and without further explanation sprang upon one end and commenced hewing at the embryo canoe; an example which Smith, the carpenter, lost no time in following. I left them at their work, and at noon sent up their dinner by an Indian boy, whom I took care to disarm of any proclivity to "crib" by stuffing him to his throat before his departure.

In the afternoon, I visited the remains of the boat, having to make a wide *detour* on a ridge of high ground to avoid being mired in the river bottom. I descried the remains of the wreck lying near the opposite bank upon the "spit" of a peninsula which the freshet had raised to the dignity of an independent island. It was covered with alders which had interrupted the descent of varieties of small and large timber, until an entanglement of waifs had piled up a barrier upon the principle of a stationary avalanche, receiving accessions of minor ones from the hilltops. The cliff from which I looked down upon the scene was not less than eighty feet high, and dominated those capricious sinuosities of the Merced which had apparently served to retain in one elbow or another a large majority of the booty brought down from the mountains. At all events I reckoned up logs enough for a bridge, let alone a new ferry-boat, and retraced my steps with corresponding serenity. . . . . If all hands worked "with a will," we should be ready to "launch" in three weeks, during which period scarce a dozen teams were likely to pass.

There was another pleasing reflection: no imaginable contingency could arise to impede our labors. There were but two freshets a year—one in winter and one in sum-

mer; the former the result of rain, and the latter of sunshine. We should have no interruptions and no distrac-
tions to divert us from our purpose. . . . .

The canoe was perfected the second day and brought
down to the ferry before the subsiding waters had uncovered the rock which usually formed a barrier to navigation
between the two crossings. I had learned the use of the
paddle while a boy, when I had spent many an hour
maneuvering a birch-bark canoe sent to me from the lakes
by my worthy friend Mr. Cashier Ridout, of Toronto.[4]
There is no method of locomotion in which you get such
immediate and visible returns for the powers and skill
expended, and strange to say, our Indians knew nothing
of "canoeing." Not having been among the northern
tribes, I am unable to say what proficiency they possess in
nautical art, but upon the three rivers with which I was
familiar in California—the Stanislaus, Tuolumne, and
Merced—I never saw an Indian bark, nor a native use
the paddle. This, I suppose, is attributable to the insig-
nificance of the streams. Necessity is the mother of invention, and in the cases which came under my eye the absence of the mother accounts for that of the child.

We established our boat-yard upon a convenient elevation of the opposite bank, not far from the island upon
which our boat had been cast away. Our anticipations were
not too sanguine, for we found, without needing recourse
to the forest, all the material required for our new craft.
Her predecessor was ruthlessly dissected with a view to
extract the spikes and bolts; and such of the floor and side
planks as might prove serviceable were carefully removed.
I spent my days at the theatre of our new creation, in
which I felt quite as much absorbed as a yacht fancier in

[4] Thomas Gibbs Ridout (1792–1861), cashier (general manager)
of the Bank of Upper Canada from 1822 until his death.

the progress of the schooner which he fondly hopes may win the prize cup of the next season's regatta. The whip and cross-cut saws were in constant requisition, and when "blown" by my own contributions to the general labor, I would sit and admire the patience and endurance of Smith and "Uncle Abe," whose average of steady work exceeded ten hours a day. I never understood the meaning of the word "top-sawyer," which I had heard used by Mr. Killaly to characterize his position at Mount Ophir,[5] until I saw the burly Smith raining down the sawdust upon the uncomplaining veteran who tugged at the lower extremity of the whip-saw. . . . .

I forgot to mention that, to spare our friends and customers the annoyance of driving their teams to our disabled crossing, immediately after the disaster I placed a sign board at the "turn-off," which notified travellers that our ferry was "closed for repairs." . . . .

At the expiration of a fortnight the hull of our ark had been put together, and in a week or ten days more she would be ready for the "ways."

Our progress had been more than satisfactory—it was marvellous. This was partly owing to the enthusiastic zeal with which our people seconded my wishes, and partly to the magnificent climate of the only country in the world of which I can say that, during a five years residence, I never closed my window, save to keep out rain, never had a fire

---

[5] This is as suitable a place as any to record the melancholy fact that as top-sawyer at Mount Ophir Killaly was not a success. His first mistake was not to recommend that the Merced Mining Company build its reduction works farther north in the valley, where there was more water and richer ore. And in his optimism he spent too much money above ground before sufficient investigation of the vein. The annual report of the trustees for 1852 said that the Mount Ophir works had been honestly managed but with "a great paucity of the established principles of business economy"—and must be shut down.

in my room, and never wore an overcoat, nor a pair of summer pantaloons.

About this time we needed sundry iron bolts, rings, and hinges, in quest of which I made a trip to Quartzburg, where we had a forge attached to the Washington quartz mill. The road had been comparatively deserted, and my welcome at Thorn Villa was multiplied by commiseration for our misfortune, tidings of which had reached there with the usual celerity of bad news. Sincere were the congratulations of my friends upon the energy with which we had turned the fruits of the freshet to account, and Col. Thorn was overjoyed when I authorized him to announce in a week the readiness of our ferry to accommodate the public. The blacksmith's work upon our bolts detained me a day and a half, during which I had time to inspect the mill and its accounts. The beneficent kobold who had showered treasures upon us during that one memorable week had not made his reappearance. The rock was getting a little more obdurate. The stampers required more frequent chilling. But we were still slightly ahead of expenses, though, unless the vein should improve, the prospect of dividends seemed as remote as the White House to Mr. Douglas.

On the afternoon of the second day I set out for home with a goodly array of bolts and pins tied to my saddle bow. The road was still slippery, and the additional weight prompted Frémont to an unusually staid and fastidious tread. The leisurely pace afforded me a chance for undisturbed reflection upon one concerted piece in our ferry opera, of which I had not yet "faced the music." . . . . it was useless to disguise the emptiness of the coffers from which the wages of our naval architects were to be dispensed. There had been no gold washing of any consequence for several weeks, and the remainder of our fall accumulations had been dispatched to pay for our winter stores. We had devoured the last and poorest of our beeves, and the Indians, after consuming, during the freshet and the weeks following, nearly all our stock of beans, had cheerfully returned to their pristine diet of acorns and grass seeds for the nonce. I could see but one solution to the problem. I must either ask Smith and Uncle Abe to share our short commons until the renewal of the spring trade (and the vigor of their appetites under such circumstances portended starvation), or draw upon San Francisco for money. The alternative, though disagreeable, seemed inevitable. However, if they were paid off, they would doubtless remain until the return of fine weather, and thus spend half their wages at the *ranche*. The loss of this contribution would increase the cost of the boat nearly fifty per cent. I knew the co-proprietor, who was shiftless and embarrassed, would be unable to supply a dollar, so I resolved upon a letter and a draft, and a lien upon her to be obtained from him for his moiety of the cost of her construction.

Such letters are unpleasant writing when addressed to a friend. They may be quite the reverse when one pulls upon a curmudgeon. Yet they are the usual consequences of remote speculations. Who has not been called upon to pay unexpected assessments upon copper shares in Lake Superior, or those in still more exalted North Carolinian undertakings? Gold mines require a bank, silver mines a reckless confidence on the part of their proprietors,[6] and even iron and coal sometimes live upon you instead of your living upon them. I have heard it audaciously asserted that here and there the cost of building a railroad exceeds the estimates, and it has been sometimes whispered in my

[6] Three years after he wrote this, Ward invested in the Gould and Curry silver mines a ten-thousand-dollar fee he had earned on a mission to Central America. Within a few months the investment was worthless.

presence that far-off steamboats occasionally diminish, in lieu of augmenting, the income of their owners. . . . .[7]

On reaching the *ranche* I found Bau-tis-ta expecting me. He had been successful in hunting; had killed an

[7] Toward the close of 1851 finances at the ferry became complicated. Business failure often leaves more documents than success; and Belt & Company was no exception, for shortly after a letter from Sam Ward had brought Drought on a visit to the Ferry, everyone in the concern was signing papers. Complete analysis of the details would employ as many attorneys as are today busy with the six-way lawsuit over the Gaines Ledge at Quartzburg, but the following summary gives the main facts.

William Howard and both of the Belts, in November 1851, took pre-emption claims of 160 acres each along the south bank of the Merced at the Ferry. Five documents dated December 15, 1851, and witnessed by Sam Ward accomplished the following: George Belt and William Howard sold their pre-emption claims to Upton Belt and Drought; Thomas Howard sold his land titles to Upton Belt; and the members of the firm signed an agreement (*a*) that William Howard should operate exclusively on the Tuolumne and should consider Upton Belt and Drought trustees of all the profits made there, (*b*) that Upton Belt and Drought should be trustees at the Merced for the liquidation of the debts of Upton Belt to Drought, (*c*) that George Belt should give all his time to buying cattle, and (*d*) that all profits should remain in the business until its debts to Drought were paid. Four days later Upton Belt granted Drought one-fourth of the establishment and its profits for $6,000 already advanced. Two weeks later, on January 2, 1852, he gave Drought a mortgage to the Merced establishment because of $18,000 Drought was then said to have advanced. Later in January, with Drought not present, Sam Ward forced the signing of two papers which gave Drought title to three-fourths of the establishment. These documents were held until the firm's condition became even worse; then they were recorded, in April 1852.

In June 1852 Drought, who by then owed $30,000 to a San Francisco banker, turned over to his creditor the mortgage to the Merced establishment that Upton Belt had given, but which would be hard to collect because Belt seems to have succeeded the month before in selling an interest in the property to an outsider. The complications eased when the ferrymen from just upstream, John Phillips elk, and having brought me what the trappers call the *depouilla,* and the Romans termed the *spolia opima,* had invited himself to supper. The meat was fat and tender, but sweet! Nevertheless it was more palatable than fried bacon, which would otherwise have been my supper, and imparted a relish to the musty ship-biscuit to which our rations were reduced. When I had finished supping, the chief burst into an uncontrollable and undignified fit of laughter. While drying his tears, he replied to my puzzled look by exclaiming that I had been eating horse! It appeared that on some occasion I had expressed repugnance for that Scythian diet, and great was his glee at my unconsciousness of the trick. Their hunters, after an absence of some days, had returned from the Tulare with several loads of meat, to the infinite delight of the tribe. My prejudice having thus been overcome, I invited him to repeat the joke as often as he should feel in the humor. . . . .

. A day or two afterwards, the heavy hinges destined for the moveable flaps at either end of the boat, as well as certain iron knees for bracing up her sides, were sent down from Quartzburg, where I had left an order with the blacksmith, who had made a "good job" of it. About the same time we received a new coil of heavy cable from below, which completed her outfit. Her seams had been caulked. The indefatigable Smith had found "fine stuff" enough among the *disjecta membra* deposited by the exhausted deluge to construct a new and graceful railing; and after an early dinner, all hands went down to launch

and his new partner named Young, bought the whole establishment late in 1853.

All told, by the end of 1853, twenty documents concerning title to the ferry and store had been signed in the little over two years since Ward and Drought first saw the place. And Henry Drought by then was, perhaps happily, dead in Central America.

her, on the twenty-third day from the accident. As the canoe held but four persons, we were an hour in "crossing" the whole party. When it came the turn of the Indians who, as I have remarked, were no adepts with the paddle, they stripped, twenty at a time, threw their clothes into the canoe, and plunging into the water pushed it over with joyous shouts and screams.

When I reached the boat-yard, Smith, on whom rested the responsibility of our success, stood at one end, axe in hand, with a look of severity and an air of determination. "Uncle Abe" had taken a similar position opposite, and I fancied discovering in his expression traces of tender regret that so lucrative a job should have reached its termination. On my arrival, they raised their axes to knock away the two last "chocks" that wedged the boat on the ways, when I announced my intention of being launched in her, having invited Lady Bau-tis-ta, and a few other princesses of the tribe, to assist at the ceremony, which, among nautical men, is considered imperfect unless graced by the presence of the fairer sex. I accordingly led the way, conducting with one hand the Princess, whose locks, dripping with her recent immersion, were, unhappily, too dark to admit of her being likened to any river or marine goddess of heathendom, although she might have stood for the picture of the baptism of Pocahontas. In the other hand I held a black bottle, with a red seal, one of my last three flasks of claret. When we had taken our positions, the word was given, the axes fell, the hull glode, at first slowly, and then with gathering swiftness until, with a plash, it smote the water, and a moment after floated amidst the frantic cheers of the crowd. I handed the bottle to the Princess, who smashed it upon the bow with such energy that the wine sprinkled the group into as many bacchanals.

And thus was launched and baptized the A-1 new ferry

A ferryboat

barge, *Never-Say-Die*. No craft ever floated more lightly upon "Omar's green water"; and few ship-wrecked mariners have touched shore with greater satisfaction than filled me as I trod her quarter-deck, of which, by-the-bye, being destined to impartial transportation from one river bank to the other, she had two! With the aid of fifty auxiliary red-skins, we warped her triumphantly up stream, the ladies still on board—half-a-dozen Cleopatras, and I the only Antony. We drew her to her berth—the new cable had been stretched—and by nightfall she was in fine running order.

My last "official act" before supper was to have the melancholy board which announced "the temporary closure of the crossing" replaced by a conspicuous effort of sign painting which acquainted "our friend and customers, and the travelling public generally, that the new and spacious barge at our ferry was now making her regular trips."

129

THERE IS one great charm in the climate of California. Its rudest winter corresponds to a rainy April on Manhattan Island, and when the rain ceases to fall, spring is upon you, like sunshine when you lower your umbrella after a shower, or the warmth of your fireside when you have left your overcoat in the entry. . . . .

A fortnight after the launch of the *Never-Say-Die*, "all the clouds that lowered on our house," all the troubles which had occasioned her creation, and the anxieties attendant upon her progress, were numbered with the buried past. Smith, the carpenter, and "Uncle Abe" had received their drafts upon our San Francisco patron and stowed them away in the recesses of their wallets with the gratifying reverence due to "certificates of deposit." The river had subsided sufficiently to entice the pick, the spade, and the pan of the Indian, and though our receipts of gold at the store were as yet but moderate, the keeper of the till remarked by way of consolation, that the dust was of unusually fine quality this season. . . . .

Did you ever go a nutting and imagine that you had completely stripped the ground of the fallen fruits of some patriarchal tree? If so, you will perhaps remember that for weeks after its pods were surrendered to the November blasts there was still very tolerable picking among the fallen leaves. To a child, the phenomenon seems inexplicable. What wonder, then, that our Indians should have imagined that the gold grew in the river like the acorns in the woods, when each year seemed to renovate the bed of the Merced with a fresh supply of the coveted spangles. I recollect a small "pocket," near a boulder on the river banks, which had been exhausted the previous autumn, until one might wash pan upon pan of the grey sand without finding the "color of gold" at the bottom of the *batea*, and which, replenished with fresh sediment by the flood, yielded apparently quite as much treasure as had been already taken out of it. Leaving to experts the elucidation of this geological mystery, I merely desire to record a fact with which most stream diggers in California must be familiar.

And this reminds me of the imperfect knowledge of our early fortune hunters, not only touching the origin of the gold deposits, but as to the stratification of the successive layers of the auripletive soil. There was a small but rich "claim" in Mariposa from which a man and his boy had washed some two thousand dollars out of the alluvium. At the bottom of the pit they came to fine sand, and the "digging" appeared to be exhausted. They accordingly sold out for a trifle to three new comers, who proceeded to excavate the sand until they came to a thick bed of coarse gravel from which they extracted nearly twice as much gold as their predecessors, and rested their labors upon a layer of marl which seemed to be the termination of the deposit. They, therefore, in turn, disposed of the claim for a small amount to a couple of sturdy delvers, who at once commenced removing the clay, several feet in thickness, and came upon a thin layer of slate, in the interstices of which they found as much gold as had been taken by both the preceding parties. Thinking that they had now struck the "bed rock," they abandoned the spot, unable to find a purchaser. Several months elapsed, during which the pit remained neglected, when a new party of prospectors, after listening to the romantic legend of the claim, resolved to break through the crust of slate at no little expense and wear and tear of gunpowder and crow-bar.

The experiment was deemed Quixotic by the community until the removal of the slate uncovered a fresh bed of mingled clay and gravel, at a distance of about twenty feet below the upper surface, whence they took in a short space of time nearly forty pounds of gold to the hand, some of the nuggets being of the size of a clenched fist, before they came to the primitive trap rock which put an end to their further investigations. I will add that in these successive layers, the gold increased in coarseness of grain in an almost geometrical ratio. . . . .

On the River of Grace, the spring of '52 fell upon us as suddenly as a crop of mushrooms . . . . The trees endued their foliage with the rapidity of practised actors between scenes, and the kingfisher sat upon the willow branch once more watching for his prey.

With spring came a new and exciting element into the uniformity of our existence. A stage was shortly to commence running from Stockton to Mariposa, and to carry a tri-weekly mail, which had hitherto been hebdomadally transported on horseback. It was important to secure its crossing at our ferry. There are Masonic ties outside of the lodge . . . . so I sent a note to Maj. Hammond at Stockton, with a request that he would do the officious for the *ranche* towards the projectors of our new line of *messageries*.

Not long after the transmission of my message, the Indians telegraphed one afternoon the approach of a "new rolling house," which was their expression for a wagon, and my glasses soon enabled me to descry one of those mountain stages which still carry travellers through the mining regions, and have multiplied on the plains like rabbits since the opening of the three overland routes to

California. There was a moment of suspense while the
vehicle was nearing the fork where our road met the trail
to Phillips' Ferry. Had Maj. Hammond got my letter?
Had he attended to its request? Had he been successful?
Five minutes more and the stage would answer these inquiries. I watched it with external composure, but inward
anxiety, and was, as all persons of experience should be,
prepared for the worst. "Huzzah!" shouted Frank the
butcher, at my elbow, "she's coming our way," and without
pausing to inquire his authority for the sex of the object
in question, I saw with satisfaction that the driver unhesi-
tatingly left the Phillips road on his left, and was coming
straight to us with the familiarity of an old friend. To use
a trite expression of those regions, "you'd better believe"
the new barge with all the force of crew we could muster
found her way to the opposite bank in a trice; she was
moored, the bridge flap lowered, a few stones picked out of
the track, so that when the equipage came through the cut
in the bluff, the Jehu remarked, as he drove triumphantly
upon the *Never-Say-Die*, that it was "as good as crossing a
bridge" to be ferried over in such style. I had ordered a
little collation of biscuit, ham and horse-hash to celebrate
the arrival of the first stage; this, and a bottle of whiskey,
both *gratis*, completed the conquest initiated by the gal-
lantry of my friend the Major. As the travellers were to
rest that night in Quartzburg, and continue their journey
to Mariposa at daybreak, I had no sooner realized the
ineffable delight of perceiving that they ignored Phillips'
ranche en passant than I dispatched an Indian courier with
a note, acquainting Col. Thorn with the approach of these
distinguished strangers, that he might be prepared to receive them with due honor and an abundance of corn cakes
and buttermilk.

This *prevenance* was not original, and I hasten to acknowledge the distinguished author from whom it was

plagiarized. This was no less a person than Herr Helworth of the Hotel de Bade, where I remember witnessing the arrival of an *estafette* one afternoon in the month of May, 1834, which threw the whole establishment into paroxysms as lively as the tumult of a Mexican *pronunciamento*. The most noble, the Marquis of Hertford (Thackeray's Lord Steyne),[1] was drawing near Heidelberg with his suite and three equipages, on his way to London for "the season." Mine host, after having drilled his company of waiters as nearly as possible to flunkeyism, dispatched a courier to Frankfort with sealed orders which he privately informed me were to apprise Sarg of the Hotel de Russie of the advent of his lordship, and to impart at the same time the interesting information he himself had just received from Hoffman, the landlord of the Erb Prinz at Carlsruhe, that "the tariff agreed upon that summer for his lordship's rooms by the innkeepers upon his lordship's route was thirty *louis d'ors* a night," a uniformity of rate at which his lordship must have been highly gratified.

Early in the forenoon of the second day after its passage up to Mariposa, the pioneer stage returned and the route was opened. The first ray of practical civilization had thus traversed our plains and flashed upon the benighted mining valleys beyond. On the same afternoon, the alternate "diligence" made its appearance, having been met by the "pioneer" at the Tuolumne and directed to the *ranche*. The driver, like a Sandy Hook pilot, handed me a newspaper a week old. Our larder being unable to afford a second collation, we confined our welcome to a jorum of whiskey.

A bargain was then struck for the ferriage, which was

[1] Thackeray is said to have modeled the Marquis of Steyne in *Vanity Fair* and *Pendennis* after the notorious Francis Charles Seymour Conway, the third Marquis of Hertford.

Staging in the mountains

fixed at a dollar, although we had a right to an extra quarter for each passenger. I knew that Dickenson, at the Tuolumne, would kick at this reduction, but he—the lucky dog!—had no opposition to contend with. The drivers, if they chose, might pocket the difference; that was no business of mine, but it was important to have two such trumpeters upon the road to blow for us and counteract any efforts which desperation might suggest to Phillips, to quicken the stagnation of his trade. It will thus be seen that the "art-of-conveyance," as is well known when it rises to the dignity of railroads and ocean steamers, must, even in the humble sphere of a ferry, have recourse to the auxiliary artifices of diplomacy. The management of stages, which is an intermediate branch between the *Never-Say-Die* and the *Great Eastern*, involves a genius *sui generis* which blends the enterprise of the common carrier with the astuteness of the horse jockey. Whenever it has been my lot to encounter, in a *negocio*, the keen wits of a stage man, I have uniformly followed the example of Capt. Scott's celebrated "coon" and "come down," when I could not get away. It was, therefore, a happy thought to enlist the sympathies and lungs of the drivers in behalf of what a distinguished Wall Street operator would have designated the "suffering interest" of our crossing.[2]

The spring, which brought us a respite from rain, and a line of stages, brought little change to the Indian *ranchería*. There was, to be sure, the additional comfort of sleeping dry within its leafy huts, but the season was not the signal for any of those labors which plant the seeds of future abundance. In the autumn, for several weeks preceding the deluge, I had admired the ceaseless activity of the crones who went forth into the forest to gather acorns, and upon the hill sides to strip the rarer grasses of their seeds, and were often several days absent before having filled their baskets. Indeed the whole duty of provisioning the *ranche*, save now and then with mustang meat, seemed to devolve upon the withered harpies of the tribe. The maidens led a life of butterfly indolence, if not luxuriance; forever sporting their brightest finery of calico and silken kerchiefs, and only condescending to the occasional exertion of washing a few pans of golden sand on a "field day."

Spring, therefore, so far from inspiring its customary joy and wonted activity, as the days waxed finer shed a growing gloom upon the faces of my dusky *protégés*. The *salmon were behind their time*, and the chiefs began to apprehend their having been scared away by the steamboats, bridges and dams of the whites between the *ranche* and tide-water. An exploring party was despatched down

[2] The other stages to Mariposa ran from Stockton easterly and then south through the towns of the Mother Lode. This new line running by way of Belt's Ferry was inaugurated in mid-April of 1852, by J. W. Whisman and F. Bonacina.

stream to ascertain the truth or the error of this surmise, and returned with the intelligence that some fishermen, several miles below, had thrown a dam across the river to serve a weir, above which the fish could not ascend to their usual spawning beds. These melancholy tidings were formally imparted to me by Bau-tis-ta and Trypoxi, with notice that it would be hard to restrain the indignation and hunger of the tribe from destroying so unjust an impediment to the arrival of the only food, save acorns, vouchsafed by nature to their people. I could neither withhold my sympathy with their irritation, nor my assent to its justice. The dilemma was both painful and perplexing. It would not do to encourage the aggrieved to take the law in their own hands against the aggressors. Justice was not yet firmly seated upon her throne in the state. There were laws, it is true, but no one to enforce them, save in San Francisco, and perhaps Sacramento, where the growth of monstrous abuses had been already checked on more than one occasion by that ever-ready "Third American Estate," the Vigilance Committee of Chief Justice Lynch. There was, accordingly, no redress short of Mariposa or Stockton, and I resolved to ride down and inspect not only the objectionable fish barrier but the parties who had built it. I found the interruption some ten miles below us. It had been started under a chaotic impression that there might be gold in that bend of the river, and an equally idiotic determination to turn it from its channel. An examination of the bed sand not having revealed the wished-for "color," the party next imagined diverting the swiftness of the local current to the propulsion of a mill wheel; but reflection having taught them that there was neither timber to saw nor corn to grind in the vicinity, they had resolved to convert their dam into a great salmon trap. They numbered about a half dozen, principally Dutchmen, no very formidable adversaries in

137

the absence of lager beer, and these poor devils had not even sauerkraut with which to preserve their nationality. I had my choice of three different "lines of country"— the mysterious dread of war-whooping savages yelling for their rightful food; the vindictive indignation of the miners on the upper river; and lastly, that species of mother wit which once prompted the keeper of a lunatic asylum, whom a maniac was urging to jump with him from the eaves of the roof to test his power of flying, to suggest that it would be a much more creditable performance to walk down and fly up. "The salmon," said I, "if unimpeded, will find their way up stream, and once above your barrier cannot retrace their steps without paying you toll; whereas, when they come in sight of this profane dam, they will be almost certain to turn tail and seek some other spawning ground on the San Joaquin. Let them pass up, for otherwise, what with savages and miners, your work will disappear some dark night, like a spider's web beneath the foot of a mule." I made sure that a party who had committed two such egregious blunders as the attempts to turn a stream which contained no gold and to erect a mill where there was nothing to grind would not be apt to foresee how much the "school" of salmon would be thinned by the up-river populations, and how worthless the exhausted "hawk's bills" would be on their way back to the sea.

I did not stop to inquire which of my arguments had prevailed, when, after a brief consultation, the Fatherlanders agreed to throw open the weir and not close it until the fish should have been running at least a fortnight. I rode back to the *rancheria* with the welcome tidings, and received the dignified acknowledgements of the chiefs and the enthusiastic plaudits of the *plebs*. A small corps of observation was detailed to watch the advent of the finny tribe, and not long after, a breathless messenger from below announced that the "monarch of the water"—the Potoyensees had never seen a whale—had made his appearance. By this time, the rocks, to which I have alluded as impeding navigation between the two ferries, had been denuded by the gradual fall of the river to its normal height, and one evening, a little after moon rise, I was invited by the Izaak Walton of the tribe to accompany him to the rapids where he hoped to take some fish. The angler carried a spear with a slender handle about six feet in length, with a sharp flint head armed with a double barb of what appeared to be stout fish bones skillfully attached by fine sinews, so that the points turned slightly inwards— a stout line was wound spirally around the lance and terminated in a small coil carried in the hand. He was attended by his son, a lad of about fourteen, who carried a basket and a couple of extra spear heads. We moved as noiselessly as though stalking red deer, and when we reached the rapids, the harpooner, motioning us to the shade of some bushes which commanded a view of his operations, advanced like a shadow to the cover of a stump, where he stood perhaps a quarter of an hour, so stock still as to seem an appendage of its trunk. Suddenly his arm was raised and the harpoon darted nearly into the middle of the river. The fish had been struck, and in a second the boy rushed in among the rocks to help secure him. There were plashes and a struggle, but the boy forced him into deep water, and the father, with a steady pull, drew him in shore; the boy, swimming after him the while and touching bottom as he approached the bank, crept up behind the struggler, until both were within a yard or so of the fisherman, when the urchin, stooping down, "scooped" the fish with his closed hands, and gave him a "flip," which tossed him on the grass where he became a prisoner. The action lasted some five minutes, and was quite exciting, though the performance of the aid-de-camp reminded me of that of the retrievers employed at Maxwell's Point in Chesapeake Bay, to bring in crippled canvasbacks. The angler, however, would have made a tip-top harpooner in the bow of a whale boat. When the barb had been cut out, I had leisure to examine the salmon, which was about twelve pounds in weight, and as plump as a Severn "grilse." I then inspected the barb, which, considering its slender proportions and elasticity of material, had stood the racket wonderfully—the only injury being the blunting of one of the points, which a knife soon sharpened anew. The next shot missed the fish, and struck the rock. The lance was hauled in, and a portion of the apex of the flint found to be broken. The fisherman sat himself down in the moonlight, and in an incredibly short time adjusted a new spear head with the dexterity of a trouter whipping on a fly. The third cast was successful, and again the retrieving biped rushed into the stream and, driving the fish towards the bank, made a landing net of his hands. A fourth cast brought a third victim ashore; but this time the barb was broken in its extraction. A cloud over the moon left too little light to adopt a new head, and I returned home towards midnight, delighted with the artistic skill of the Indian harpooner.

The next day and night, all the fishermen of the tribe resorted to the rapids, but the "catch" was small; the old men shook their heads, and had they been born in Connaught would have said: "Bad luck to the ugly dam." The cavaliers of the tribe started off the following day to a *sault* below the Dutch obstruction, and after an absence of a week or more—during which the store, despite the arrival of a load of new and attractive wares from below, took in but little gold dust—returned with several quintals of dried fish, which, so far as I could judge, was very impartially distributed among the people of the *rancheria*.

I think it was toward the end of March that the co-proprietor, while sitting on my bench shortly after dark, pricked up his ears at some distant sound, listened a moment and then exclaimed: "There's a death at the *rancheria*. I hear the wail!" Curious to witness an Indian wake . . . . I followed him to the village, which had lately been replaced in the valley whence its inmates had been driven by the freshet. In the open air the sounds of lamentation seemed to ascend spirally in the distance, and as we drew near the huts, I recognized the same mournful dirge which I had noticed when the unbelieving crones persisted in chanting the requiem of the truant Sacate. Threading the dog-infested paths of the village, we slackened our pace so as to approach the house of mourning with such manifestations of respectful sympathy as are always due to the greatest misfortune next to birth. The moon had not yet risen, and it was only by the light of the smoldering embers that we perceived the dusky form of a squaw performing a forlorn *pas seul* in cadence with a lugubrious chant which commenced with a shrill wail, and fell in minor triplets until it reached a "sensible note," which was repeated with an intervening appoggiatura. The voice then rebounded, as if from the ground, to the initial wail, and renewed its descent, until, like a ball at the end of its tether, it was once more caught on cup or point, and again released. The accompanying dance was a series of violent revolving jumps with closed feet, executed with an energy so nearly approaching fury that one's eyes involuntarily sought the form of the prostrate foe the Pythoness was trampling in the dust. The dance and chant grew in progressive violence, until the wail became a shriek and the phases of the *cadenza* as sharply accentuated as the tap of a drum. At the end of each stanza, I heard groans issuing from within the hut, and when familiarized with the obscurity, my eyes detected a row of old men sitting on the ground, with their hands clasped below their knees, upon which their chins rested. When one Pythoness had danced and sung to exhaustion, she sank prostrate among the female mourners, another of whom instantly took her place and continued the Runic lament.

From time to time accessions of women came in singly, caught the step, and joined in the chant of the performer, when the two would vie in desperation, until, with giddy heads and scarcely audible sobs, they in turn fell to the ground. In a corner of the hut, I, at length, discovered a mysterious package, which proved to be the corpse ready for sepulture. Learning that the wake was to last all night, I returned home, leaving word with a lad to call me privately when the mourners should proceed to the funeral obsequies. From him I learned that the deceased brother had been ailing a considerable while, and had died of consumption. Long after "turning in," I was kept awake by the owl-like "*tu hu*" of the distant lullaby, and only fell asleep when I had succeeded in resolving to reserve my sympathy and reflections for the morrow.

Although apprized by the co-proprietor of the secrecy observed in the performance of their exequies, I felt confident that my friendly presence would not be regarded as an intrusion by the Indians, and my curiosity was not a little heightened by learning that the Potoyensees practiced incineration according to the rite of the ancients.

Shortly after daybreak, the lad scratched at my window, and when I came out of the house, he pointed to a clump of trees on the bluff, to which I could see an Indian file slowly repairing in the distance. I hastened thither, and reached the spot with the end of the procession. We all took seats against the trees which enclosed a natural clearing about forty feet square; the men and women upon opposite sides, after the fashion of the Quakers. In the centre, the body lay upon three logs, which crossed two

142

"sleepers." A stout Indian, with whose face I was not familiar, acted as master of ceremonies, made several trips into the grove and returned with armfuls of light wood. When he had thus procured a sufficient supply of fuel, he made a sign, and the men of the tribe, rising one by one, each deposited a trifling token upon the body. The women followed in turn, and were more prodigal of beads, hand-kerchiefs, and even valuable objects, for a blanket and if I do not err, a *sarape* were added to the pile. The gloomy-looking official then waved all back to their places, and stowing some kindling wood between the sleepers, and heaping up the pyre with fuel of the same description, applied the torch; at the first crackling of the flames, the wail burst forth anew from the sorrowing women, and was answered by the responsive moans of the other sex.

The scene was sad beyond description, and after mar-velling at the rapidity with which the body was consumed by the flames which transported me in memory to the earliest description I had read of a funeral pile, that of Patroclus—and the last—that of Shelley, I examined critically the circle of mourners, whose grief, though more subdued than at its first explosion the night previous, was no less woe-begone and, I am not ashamed to say, infec-tious. The only external emblems of mourning were the poor women's blackened faces, and it was heart-melting to realize the indigence of a race too poor to indicate their bereavements by the slightest change of dress. Although when witnessing the removal of the *ranchería* I had ob-served the paucity of their personal possessions, I did not fully comprehend until I assisted at this mortuary cere-mony that a pocket handkerchief would hold the worldly chattels of any woman of the tribe. Perhaps their hope-less and lonely wretchedness enhanced a sorrow which I never saw more sincere beneath the most lugubrious weeds of civilization. The master of ceremonies stirred the pyre, from time to time adding fresh sticks to the flames. The cremation was accomplished in less than an hour—when the mourners retired and left the gloomy official to gather up the ossuary relics, which, placed in a basket, would be deposited at night in the Potoyensee necropolis, the site of which was carefully concealed not only from the whites but from all the young people of the tribe.

AS THE SEASON advanced, and the travel over
the ferry and the trade of the store gave tokens of growing prosperity, I fell into that state of dreamy indifference
which is not unlike the languor induced by a sojourn in
the tropics. The establishment went on like clock-work.
We had once more a drove of cattle pasturing in the tolerably grassy bottom, and had remitted upwards of one
hundred and fifty ounces of gold dust to San Francisco,
to pay for old and purchase new supplies. The novelty
of the stage had lost its bloom, and I frequently kept my
room, or neglected to come in from the shelter of a favorite
willow, when the horn announced its approach. I was absorbed in "Bleak House," then drawing near its conclusion,
and the month intervening between the numbers seemed
interminable as the plot thickened. Nor should it be a
matter of surprise that Sir Leicester and Lady Dedlock,
Mr. Tulkinhorn, Mr. Guppy, Miss Flittle, and even the
detestable Smallweeds—I quote from memory, not having opened the book since I devoured it on the Merced[1]
—were personages of more attractive interest than the
group of whites and the clusters of savages around me.
I had recourse to the saddle to quicken the torpor stealing
over me, but I found in solitary horsemanship something
worse than the Horatian "care behind the cavalier"—the

[1] Memory failed in the detail of three names: Mr. Tulkinghorn,
Miss Flite, Smallweed.

145

gloomiest remembrances of the past, with no gleams of light in the future to enliven their melancholy retrospective. I would have given the world had it been my property, for even an *ignis-fatuus* to mislead me. But in the broad light of the sunny spring days upon the River of Grace, "those children of the mist," the illusions, no longer obeyed the summons of fancy. . . . .

Seven or eight months before, I languished for repose, and now I languished, in repose, for activity. In truth, there were no more kingdoms to conquer, unless I enlisted in the great Quartz Crusade, which required resources that I neither possessed nor felt the energy to solicit, for nothing is truer than the Spanish proverb: "It needs a mine to work a mine." . . . .[2]

[2] Sam Ward did not avoid the Quartz Crusade entirely; on October 20, 1851, he shared with fourteen others the discovery of the Franklin Vein. That discovery probably grew out of his association

About this time, either to relieve the monotony of the *ranche* or to entice me back to the haunts of civilization, Providence showered upon the river the unexpected blessing of a stage load of visitors—friends from San Francisco on their way partly to see the mines and partly myself. The merriest of them, Dr. Bowie, who unites refinement, breeding and scholarship to wonderful Esculapian sagacity,[3] and Maj. Sibley, for whom every day is a Fourth of July,[4] were bent upon an instructive "lark" in the mountains, whither I joyfully consented to pilot them. The party were my guests for a couple of days, during which I longed for a Caleb Balderstone[5] to remedy

with the Washington Vein, for the Franklin was at the end of the Washington, and many, perhaps all, of the discoverers were interested in the older claim. But by spring, Ward was more on his own, for on March 24, 1852, with seven men whose names have appeared nowhere else during this examination of his life, he claimed by right of discovery a quartz vein lying southwest of the Mariposa-Stockton Road.

[3] Augustus J. Bowie (1815–1887) was a cultivated man whose attractive house, which had been prefabricated and shipped around the Horn and in which he collected a large library, was said to be the gathering-place of the more intellectual Californians of the 'fifties. Jessie Frémont, in a passage already quoted, recalled that Dr. Bowie was in the group of San Franciscans she had found most entertaining during 1849.

[4] Alexander H. Sibley and Sam Ward had been together in San Francisco as members of the First California Guard, in which Sibley was especially active. Directories of 1850–53 described Sibley as an importer and merchant. He knew the Southern Mines before Ward did, for in February 1851, with Thomas Thorn, Joseph Tivy, and Benjamin S. Lippincott, he recorded the discovery of a quartz claim on the west bank of Maxwell Creek. In June 1852, this time with five others who included Ward's "principal," Henry Drought, he recorded discovery of another Mariposa County vein. Years after Sam Ward left California he dedicated one of his poems in *Lyrical Recreations* to Sibley.

[5] The faithful servant in Scott's *The Bride of Lammermoor*.

147

by his ingenuity the deficiencies of the larder. I luckily had beef to offer them. A month earlier they would have found nothing but mustang meat. Reserving my stories, like Madame de Staël, for the desserts, I kept my guests on foot or in the saddle from morning until night, so as to beget that best of sauces for a simple diet—appetite. But this amount of exercise also engendered thirst, not so easily quenched by my two surviving bottles of claret. A legend had therefore to be invented to impart a flavor to the indifferent whiskey of the establishment. It was my custom, at all seasons, to commence the day by a plunge in the river, which at the time of their visit had swollen a little with the first melting of spring snow in the Sierra. The temperature of the water sustained through the shady mountain passes meandered by the Merced did not exceed 40° Fahrenheit. The morning after their arrival, the air being balmy and spring like, all hands gladly accepted the proposed luxury of a bath. To prevent the premature discovery of the deception, it was agreed, at my suggestion, that we should all plunge in together, schoolboy fashion; and no schoolboys robbing an orchard ever got over fences with greater rapidity when suddenly alarmed than that with which the whole party, with yells and shrieks which might have been heard two miles, escaped from the Arctic bath—with the exception of the Doctor, who, with a certain professional decorum and the imperturbable coolness with which the members of his profession mask their dismay when they have tied the wrong artery, struck out bravely once or twice, and then landed with grave dignity, pronouncing it the most exquisite bath he had enjoyed in his life, because it had not left a particle of sensibility upon the surface of his body.

The Indians contributed not a little to the entertainment of my visitors. There was, first, the gold washing to be inspected; next, the *rancheria*; and towards evening, the lively excitement of their trade at the store. There was always (when we had any ourselves) a small supply of beef for sale to the opulent epicures of the tribe, and I remember the Dr.'s amusement at seeing old Trypoxi cheapen a cut, pay for it, retire to a corner by himself, and furtively devour all the fat with an air of intense relish, after which he carried home the lean meat to his spouse— this, the Dr. thought, was reversing the old story of Jack Sprat. There can be no harm in adding that a passion for uncooked fat was universal among the men of the tribe, a fact which I submit in the hope that it may be a new revelation to my dyspeptical friends.

On the afternoon of the second day, we had games, races, and an archery contest, with suitable prizes for the winners. Although I rarely saw them use the bow for any practical purpose, their arrows never missed a dime, and their skill as marksmen warranted the hypothesis that before the American occupation reduced them to the limits of reservations these children of the forest must have been constantly in practise. On the morning of the third day my *cavallada* sufficed to carry the whole party up to Quartzburg, where the unexpected accession of guests taxed the elastic hospitality of Thorn Villa to its utmost capacity. Our hostess' buttermilk proved an attractive novelty even to these *gourmets* of San Francisco, and when we had scoured the different veins of the valley, and exhausted the attractions of the Washington mine and mill, we returned to a rustic supper, hailed with a frantic delight, in which I participated although such joy was a melancholy commentary upon the short commons of my poor *ranche*. The moon rose betimes, teamsters and mining captains came in, the benches of the long supper table were transferred to the porch, and the lively interchanges of question and answer, of anecdote and adventure, would not have discredited the evenings at Fort Laramie or the nocturnal re-unions at an Eastern *caravanserai*. The beds in California hostelries of that date were a rude imitation of those "standees" which, prior to the opening of the present four distinct routes to Boston, used to infest the dining cabins of the large Sound steamers of the days of yore. One of our party, my old friend, William Sim, of Glasgow,[6] disliking the closeness of our sleeping quarters, established, early in the evening, a pre-emptive claim to a grass hammock that swung in the shade of two contiguous trees near the house, by placing in it his blankets. When the *tertulia* broke up, he repaired with satisfaction to his airy couch, when he was soon the happiest sleeper of the party. His dreams, alas, whether golden or rose-colored, were of short duration; the restless spirit of mischief was rarely quiet in Sibley, who prompted one of the old miners to arouse the sleeper with the inquiry whether his revolver was loaded, "for the 'bars' were about, and two nights before had stolen a mutton hung out to cool." Sim sung out lustily for a large-sized army revolver in the holsters of one of the party, and professed delight at the prospect of a tussle with a "grizzly." We bade him "good night," with commendations of his chivalrous bravery. Meanwhile, Sibley, whose stentorian voice did not need, like Roscius' in presence of his audience of ten thousand Romans, a flute to sustain it, crept stealthily around the base of the hill into a thicket in a gorge not a hundred yards beyond the hammock. Confident the apprehension awakened in his mind would not fail to interfere for some time with the renewal of Sim's slumbers, he waited nearly half an hour before uttering a deep growl, premonitory of a roar, which must have surprised

[6] William Sim and Sam Ward were together in 1849 as two of the signers of the Preamble to the Constitution of the First California Guard. And according to San Francisco legal records they had real estate dealings together two years later.

any four-footed gentleman within hearing. At the third repetition of the ominous sound, accompanied by a travelling through the bushes, and a crackling of the dried brambles, we heard the sharp rap of Sim at the door of the villa. He said, "I find it ower cauld out here in the dew; I think I'll sleep in the house after all." Though convulsed with laughter, we feigned drowsiness, and rated him soundly for disturbing our slumbers. We, however, stowed him away in the bunk left vacant by Sibley, who passed a delightful night in the deserted hammock.

On the morrow we visited Mr. Killaly, and consumed a day very charmingly amidst the marvels and beauties of Bear Valley; and after touching at Mariposa returned to Quartzburg, the adventure of Sim and the grizzly contributing all the while such a fund of hilarity that I have no other recollection of those stages of our Brundusian journey. A melancholy surprise awaited Maj. Sibley of Thorn Villa. In the confusion of our start—it being the custom of every traveller in California to saddle his own nag—he carried off some one else's saddle—a "Hope tree," invaluable to its owner, who had bestridden it all the way overland from Texas; and what made the matter worse, he had not brought it back! Here was a pretty mess! The owner, although in a hurry to be off, had awaited patiently his return, and his disgust upon finding that the Major had unwittingly suffered it to be exchanged by some "knowing one" at the Hotel in Mariposa—where the substitution must have occurred—can better be conceived than described. The Major was *non-plussed*. It would have been easy to apologize for the inadvertence of taking it away, but there was no reparation for not returning it; still, he could not give utterance to his own intense vexation in the presence of the sufferer, and I remember his taking me aside to pour into my ear, privately, the assurance of his contempt for all saddles, particularly for those made by an infernal humbug named Hope; and winding up with emphatic imprecations upon the State of Texas, its annexation, President Polk, the Battle of San Jacinto and Davy Crockett. After having relieved himself of his irritation, he recovered his composure, and we returned to the Villa to consult what was the next best thing to be done.

A wood-cut, which appeared in the London *Illustrated News* shortly before the Crimean war, giving a sketch of a Council of War in the Emperor's Cabinet at the Tuileries, at which Lord Raglan and Marshal St. Arnaud were tracing out positions on a large map spread before his majesty, always reminded me of the grave deliberations instituted on that occasion. . . . . A rude sketch was made of the various mining trails which radiated from the town of Mariposa, and to the dismay of the Major, what with Horse-Shoe Bend, Fine Gold Gulch, Greaser Gulch, and the numerous "bars" and "forks" to which his attention was called, they exceeded in number the points of the compass; with the pleasing addition that the greater portion of them lay over hills from one to three thousand feet high. Having mastered this little lesson in mountainous geography, he called for a horse, resolved to retrace his steps and find the saddle, when it suddenly occurred to him that he had no means of recognizing it, if he should happen to see it. The owner, however, assured him that it was well known in the mines, which were full of Texans, no one of whom could mistake the pinchbeck of other saddles for the gold of Hope.

Leaving the Major to pursue his way to Mariposa, we returned to the River of Grace, whither Mrs. Thorn had kindly despatched a keg of buttermilk for the supper of my guests, who took the stage for home on the morrow, enlivened and invigorated by their adventures in the mining region.

Shortly after their departure, I determined upon a

trip to Col. Frémont's *ranche* upon the Mariposa, about twenty miles distant. I only remember the ride thither as a pleasant jaunt in lovely weather overhead, and the annoyance of being stalled once or twice in treacherous quagmires where the rains of winter still lingered under foot. In many of the little pools upon the unfrequented road, we found wildfowl—particularly teal—resting a day in their migration to feed upon the tender grasses of the season. They were so tame as to suffer me to come within twenty yards of them, and my revolver secured us an improvised bait by the wayside. I remember at one shot surprising two of them out of existence. My companions on this excursion were a brother of the co-proprietor,[7] of whom perhaps more anon, and White Elliott,[8] a mountain

---

[7] On December 15, 1851, the partners in Belt & Company had agreed that Upton Belt's brother, George, should "devote his exclusive attention to the purchase of cattle for the concern." He was then only twenty-four but already had been one of the chief merchants of Stockton as well as alcalde. He had made a fortune there but seems to have lost much of it subsequently and to have moved his family to a ranch not far from the mouth of the Merced. He was murdered in 1869 at Stockton.

[8] White Elliott is a difficult man to trace in the records of the West. Bayard Taylor, accompanied by Lieutenant Beale, met him at Belt's store in Stockton in 1849; and two years later, in November 1851, he carried the chain for a survey establishing George Belt's pre-emptive right to land on the Merced near the Ferry. Bayard Taylor said of the Stockton meeting: "While waiting in the tent of Mr. Belt, the alcalde of the place, I made acquaintance with two noted mountaineers—Mr. William Knight, the first man who followed the track of Lewis and Clark, on the Columbia River, and White Elliott, a young Missourian, who for ten years had been rambling through New Mexico and the Rocky Mountains. The latter had been one of Lieut. Beale's men on the Gila, and the many perils they then shared gave their present meeting a peculiar interest. Elliott, who, young as he was, had undergone everything that could harden and toughen a man out of sensibility, colored like a young girl; his eyes were wet and he

man well known as having been the attendant of Col. Frémont in one and of Lieut. Beale[9] on several marches of exploration, who had been recently attached, in some "many-sided" capacity, to our establishment. He was as fair-haired as a Northman, with brilliant black eyes, and great cheeriness of spirit and of manner, who had seen enough of hardship "to know when he was well off." When in the saddle, he was a jolly and an eternal talker, every jolt of his mule or curvette of his horse appearing to shake out of him some reminiscence of his past life and adventures. He had enjoyed the distinguished privilege of hunting for a whole season in company with "Old Bill Williams" of mountain celebrity, immortalized by Ruxton as the only trapper who was sure to find his way to *cache* no matter how numerous the hordes of hostile Indians around him.[10] At the end of that season they were "snowed in" among the Wind River Mountains, having had their animals stolen by the Indians. They had been two days out of provisions, and had only one remaining charge of

scarcely found voice to speak. I had many opportunities of seeing him afterwards and appreciating his thorough nobleness and sincerity of character."

[9] Edward Fitzgerald Beale (1822–1893), as an officer in the Navy, crossed the continent several times in the period between 1847 and 1849, on one trip bearing official news of the California gold discovery.

[10] George F. Ruxton described "Old Bill" Williams in chapters vii and ix of *Life in the Far West,* which appeared first as a serial in *Blackwood's Magazine* during 1848 and was published as a book the next year. Bernard DeVoto, in *The Year of Decision: 1846,* considers Ruxton's description of Williams and his associates to be the first real portrayal of mountain men.

"Old Bill" was William Sherley Williams, who was born in North Carolina in 1787 and arrived in the West about 1825. After almost a quarter-century of trapping and exploration, he was killed by Indians in 1849 while trying to retrieve equipment cached by Frémont's strange fourth expedition, which he had accompanied.

ammunition, which was in Elliott's pouch.[11] Their prospects were gloomy enough. Williams, nearly exhausted by fatigue, cold, and hunger, had betaken himself to the shelter of a hollow rock, and Elliott was tramping the hills in pursuit of any living thing, even a wolf or a *coyote*, when he caught sight of a rabbit, which, on being pursued, ran into the hollow of a log. The little creature was too insignificant to waste his last charge upon; and stopping up one end of his retreat, he attacked him through the other with his ramrod fastened to the muzzle of his rifle. A soft obstacle and a faint cry apprised him of an easy victory, and turning up the end of the log, poor "bunny" dropt out, and was carried to the relief of Williams. They devoured it raw, I believe skin and all, and felt strong enough to grope towards the prairie, where the next day a crippled buffalo received Elliott's surviving bullet and feasted them into sufficient condition to reach a tolerably distant camp, whence, after sojourning the winter, Elliott accompanied a troop of filibusters into Mexico. If my memory serves me, he subsequently effected a junction with our army, and served as an M.D. (mule driver) until taken prisoner and sent into the interior with a batch of fellow captives. The treatment they received was so vile a cross between insult and starvation that he and five others, recovering their arms, made good their escape and "put out" on a bee-line for the nearest Texan frontier. Their sufferings on this march, over barren and volcanic hills, after a day or more without water, and having to kill for food the animals they had borrowed from their captors, are unsurpassed in the annals of wandering hardship. One by one his companions died by the wayside of famine, thirst, and exhaustion, and

---

[11] This was fortunate for Elliott—if Kit Carson was right in saying that with food gone no man should walk in front of Williams.

Elliott was left alone with a single comrade, whose endurance kept pace with his own. He alluded with a sigh to the stern necessity which compelled them to leave their companions as they dropped, their own lives being a question of time and motion. When they at length came in sight of grass first, and then water, they had been dragging on their weary steps three days without food or drink. . . . . His companion could not restrain his avidity, which nearly cost him his life; but White, more experienced in such vicissitudes, was nearly three hours in sipping, perhaps, a quart. He then arose with the courage of a lion, and made for a grove from which he saw the curl of smoke ascending. It was the modest abode of a Mexican *ranchero*, whose commiseration at his emaciated aspect was manifested by the utmost kindness and hospitality. He administered to White a moderate portion of meat from the coals, and then ordering horses, they returned to bring in his companion, whom they found writhing in the agonies of distension. So severe had been their trial that a fortnight elapsed before they recovered their strength sufficiently to find their way to the settlements.

The sun must have been two hours high when we hove in sight of the River Mariposa, a narrow and shallow creek which at a few miles below our crossing is lost in the sands by the want of sufficient volume to reach the San Joaquin, to which are tributary the other streams over which my narrative has led me.

Our first *coup d'oeil* was from the determination of a long and gradually sloping spur from one of the hills on our left. The plain was cheerful with luxuriant grass, dotted here and there with timber. About half a mile to the right, a capacious tent stood among the alders that fringed the creek on either side, and a mile or so beyond we saw a log cabin with a couple of out-houses, which proved to be the residence of Col. Frémont's overseer,

The town of Mariposa

Mr. Starnes.[12] I forgot to mention that the object of our trip was to increase our stock of beeves, and we were overjoyed at descrying, in advance of us, quite a herd of California cattle. Shortly after we struck the meadows, some half-dozen *vaqueros* made their appearance, driving with shouts and gambols a lassoed two-year-old heifer, just singled out of the drove, apparently for their supper. White Elliott, rising in his stirrups, gave them a "view-halloo," and setting spurs to his horse, rode at the troop with furious haste. We quietly turned our horses' heads towards the tent in the direction of which the horsemen were moving. Having the shorter side of the triangle to traverse, we intersected their path in season to witness the *coup de grace* given to the victim, and the skinning and butchering, which were accomplished with wonderful celerity. Meanwhile, Elliott had gathered brushwood and built a most scientific mountain fire, the virtue of which consists in the rapid production of the greatest possible surface of clear live coals. He then rushed into the tent and emerged with a bag of salt, after which he whittled two or more willow forks, or rather skewers. By this time the dressing was over, and all hands were invited to carve for themselves. My henchman lost no time in slicing off several pounds of *bonnes bouches*, which were immediately transferred to the embers. I imagined that his copious provision was destined for both of us; this illusion was, however, dispelled when White, perceiving my inactivity, warned me to cut for myself, the trapper law being that each must be his own cook. The *vaqueros* very politely supplied my wants, and I was soon, like an Irish emigrant in a packet ship, struggling for my portion of our cooking range, which I only obtained when Elliott's first rasher

---

[12] The text misspelled this name; Frémont's overseer was Edward S. Sterns (or Stearns).

was ready for his white teeth. For the next two hours, I saw such gormandizing as you read of in Ulysses' description of the supper of the Cyclops. The rage for the meat resembled the madness of intoxication, and as for Elliott, he looked like a cannibal, his face and hands besmeared with blood and pinguidity. There was no bread—the meat was tough, and my appetite soon satisfied. Remounting, I rode to the house, which, though quite capacious for the period, had but one furnished room, in which I found the overseer making his own coffee. I recollect our conversation turned upon agriculture, to which that portion of the *ranche* had been destined by its proprietor; and at sunset I returned to the tent to pass the night with the *capataz*, who alone had charge of the disposal of the cattle we desired to purchase. I found some of the party still cooking rashers and eating them, though with diminished ferocity. The fire was kept up during the night, and whenever I chanced to wake, I perceived one or more of the cannibals renewing their attentions to the beef of which, though it must have weighed at least one hundred and fifty pounds, there was not more than enough left for our breakfast on the morrow, when, having made our bargain for twenty head of steers, we returned to the Merced.

The process of digesting at least a dozen pounds he had devoured calmed for a wonder the loquacity of Elliott during our homeward ride.

THE SECOND DAY after our return from Fré-
mont's *ranche*, the *capataz*, attended by a couple of *vaqueros*, made his appearance on the brow of Mount Savage, driving the twenty cattle of our purchase. The arrival
of the drove created as profound a "sensation" in the
Indian camp as the unexpected interpellations of an opposition deputy in the French Chambers. Its inmates appeared to think the surprise as agreeable as it was deserved,
and no circus company entering a remote village were ever
scrutinized with glances of greater curiosity and delight.
In this respect I must pay to those children of nature,
whose dusky forms now flit before the eye of memory, the
tribute due to the simplicity of their sources of happiness.
They possessed as a nation the rare merit of uniformity.
. . . . In fact, with the exception of Feliz, and on a sub-
sequent occasion, Bau-tis-ta, I do not remember an incon-
sistent Indian in the whole tribe.[1] The scale of their joys
was confined to the restricted gamut of gradations between

[1] In speaking of Bautista here, Ward probably referred to what the
Stockton Journal reported as a "somewhat tragical occurrence which took
place on the Merced river, on the 19th May [1852]. Some Indians,
among whom was the Chief, Baptiste, who distinguished himself in the
Mariposa War, had a feast, and Baptiste, becoming intoxicated, un-
sheathed his sword, and for some cause unknown to our correspondent,
plunged it through his wife's body, causing almost instant death. She
was a good looking squaw, aged about twenty. Baptiste, it was said,
had left for Stockton . . . . on Saturday last, we had an introduction.
. . . . He remained in town a day or two."

famine and repletion. For the females, during the brief years of their unemployed gaiety and girlhood, an occasional plagiary, in silk or cotton, from the rainbow; for the men, a horse and saddle, *sombrero* and *calzoneros* constituted, next to plenteous food, the sum of their felicity. Morally, their humor was the reflection of your own; they were rarely out of temper, but enjoyed a jest with the relish of a sailor making his first appearance in the third tier after a three years cruise.

The arrival of these sleek additions to the two or three meagre surviving bullocks of our herd procured me the honor of an immediate visit of congratulation from Prince Trypoxi, to whose adoration of raw adipose I have already alluded. An alarming rumor had reached his ears that we contemplated disposing of the lean kine before having recourse to the plumper strangers. I pleaded guilty, and gave him what seemed sound reasons for this decision. He overthrew with force and ingenuity the sophistry of my argument. " . . . . A month more of pasture would add to their quality and weight; it was therefore an economy to fatten them, and on the other hand, it was wise to eat the new comers, lest the difference or inferiority of our grass might make them lose their fat. In *his* household they always ate the best first, and thus always had the best." There was no controverting the logic of these positions; the fattest of the beeves felt the axe on the morrow. . . . . .

The *vaqueros* and their captain rode home so soon as the latter had weighed and bagged the stipulated price in gold dust. To them a canter of twenty additional miles, after two days in the saddle, was less of a task than, to a sportsman, the return home from a day's shooting. The lives of that class of Mexicans are even more monotonous than the lights and shadows of Indian existence; their only excitement being the horse, the lasso, and the bullock,

A miner, by Charles Nahl

and a supper of *carne con cuero*, with a cigarito their only supplementary enjoyment. The Indian endured greater hardships, but also experienced greater compensating joys. The delirium of "treasure trove" often fired his brain, and the hope of finding it often sustained him through days of patient toil. . . . .

About this time, I undertook the business of mining "on my own hook," and went daily into the river with the Indians, at first feigning a spirit of pleasantry which might cover my retreat should the joke become painful, and subsequently continuing the pursuit as if in sportive rivalry with my dusky comrades. But, though simulating levity, I was never more in earnest. . . . . The scene of our labors was a shoal in the middle of the stream, a little more than waist deep, where the practice was to sink the pan, scoop into it with a horn spoon mud or gravel from the bottom, and when filled, take it ashore and wash out the

earth, when the specific gravity of the gold deposited it
in the lowest strata. It was easy enough to collect the
materials, but their levigation was quite another affair.
The process had to be accomplished sitting on one's heels
and submerging the *batea* in the water, where by a series
of rapid "revolutions and counter-revolutions" it was
whirled to and fro, like the balance wheel of a watch. . . . .

The aptitude of the savages—men, women and children—for this delicate mechanical operation surpassed any
exhibition I witnessed of the skill of white miners; and
was only equalled by the handiness of the Mexican ad-
venturers to be met with on almost every stream in the
Southern mines. Despairing to attain anything like this
dexterity, I formed a league with two or three young
shavers of the tribe, who gladly undertook, on shares, the
beneficiation of the results of my delvings. This industrial
caprice lasted nearly a fortnight, at the expiration of which
I found myself, by the gold scales, a little over fifteen
dollars richer than before. On one or two days our efforts
had been encouraging, and each night I had stowed away,
with closed eyes, the little representative of the day's exertion. The grand total was a grievous disappointment. The
glittering spangles, magnified by the trouble needed to
separate them, had towards the last got to look almost as
large as ounces when lying upon the fine black sand at the
bottom of the pan!

My next employment, as gold washing did not pay,
was agriculture. During the construction of the *Never-
Say-Die*, I had noticed a nice bit of soil, nearly opposite
our improvised "ship yard," distinguished by a luxuriance
of its grass from the thinner pasture of the valley. Thither
I repaired one morning, with spade and hoe, resolved upon
kitchen gardening; the only seeds in my possession being
those of melons and turnips. I was attended by my body-
guard of urchins, to whom, like . . . . Mars of old to

the first children of men, I proposed imparting the rudiments of tillage. . . . .

Our spades turned up a rich brown loam, and by nightfall of the first day a tolerably large patch was ready for the rake. The miniature garden was soon laid out in symmetrical beds, and the seeds planted. The trees in the bottom land, on the river bank, supplied us branches with which my little *peons*, skilled in Potoyensee cottage architecture, readily constructed a hedge to exclude cattle and horses, and I had, at length, something besides the *dénouement* of "Bleak House" to dream of in the future. Nothing enlivens a walk like an object at the end of the perspective, and I visited this new hope morning and evening and examined each time, with impatient solicitude, the vicinity of the small stakes. . . . . The earth soon fulfilled its promise, and our tender crop struggled to the light with great irregularity, as though not quite at home in the strange soil, the surface of which soon became parched by the unceasing sunshine; when the youngsters were again in requisition as water carriers. I gave them to understand that, as in our gold washings, one-half the produce was to be theirs, and inflamed their imagination with pictures of the luscious fruits in store for them. . . . .[2]

Another of my out-door amusements was pistol practice. No one walked a rod in that region without a revolver in his belt, and it seemed absurd to carry the weapon without learning to use it. My nerves, braced up by a life of exercise in the open air and not unhinged by conviviality or late hours, had seconded my efforts to acquire steadiness

[2] According to John Lothrop Motley, a fellow-student with Ward at George Bancroft's Round Hill School in the 1820's, each boy there was assigned a garden for corn, radishes, and melons. Perhaps Ward succeeded in passing on whatever horticulture he had learned from Bancroft, for a traveler visiting the Merced a few months after Ward left it reported that the Indians were growing "a fine crop" of melons.

of hand and precision of aim; and I remember a trial of skill that spring with an itinerant Mexican who challenged me for a wager of an ounce, which easily joined the little treasure I had previously extracted from the River of Grace.

One afternoon, toward sundown, a strange vehicle was announced as on its way to our crossing. The Indian scouts declared it unlike any "rolling house" they had yet seen, and shortly after, one of Adams & Co.'s magnificent express wagons was drawn by four splendid bays upon the *Never-Say-Die*. This was a great improvement upon the stage which had been our first herald of civilization, and the sight of it soon emptied the *rancheria* of its curious and inquisitive denizens. In addition to Billy White, the brave-looking Vermont Jehu who held "the ribbons," the equipage contained Mr. I. C. Woods, manager, and subsequently a partner, of that then eminent and useful concern, and one of its employees. I little dreamed, when the light and active little man shook hands with me and bespoke our "bridal stateroom" for the night, that the future had in store for us vicissitudes, and associations to which I recur with unalloyed satisfaction. It was his first visit to our part of the country, which he came to inspect after having extended the branches of the house throughout the northern mines, with the view of satisfying himself whether the new mining kingdoms above us were worthy of conquest.[3] The luggage of the travellers, consisting of several

[3] Isaiah C. Woods (1824–1880) was manager and subsequently president of Adams & Company, which carried on the largest express and banking business in California, partly because of his energy and skill. His success lasted until 1855, when it dramatically ended: early in February of that year two newspapers were urging him to run for United States Senator; twenty days later most of San Francisco vilified him because of the failure of his company. In August he slipped aboard the *Audubon*—some said he dressed as a woman—and sailed for Sydney. Later he went to Europe and New York, and to Texas

black leather bags, was transferred to the stranger's dormitory, with the exception of two weighty ones which were placed behind the counter with a circumspection intensified by the throng of peering Indians, whose animated presence did not justify the apprehension it had inspired. Our meat was fortunately fat, although my friend has since assured me that it was as tough as India rubber, and with hot biscuit and very fair coffee the travellers contrived to make a supper. They retired early, and I sat up later than usual, reading a volume from their roving library, which I should be compelled to surrender on the morrow. Before going to bed, I went to look for my pistol, which I had left in the guest chamber. The heavy breathing of the sleepers, who lay upon their blankets on the floor (our dormitory had neither beds nor bunks, though carpeted with china matting), ceased at my second foot-fall, and while groping in a corner for my revolver, a couple of "clicks" drew my attention in the direction of the sound, where the dim light from the ante-chamber through the open door was reflected by the barrels of a pair of levelled revolvers in the hands of Mr. Woods and the employee, who bore the appropriate name of Colt. Having transferred their bags of coin to their pillows, they had fallen asleep, dreaming of Malay pirates and Dyaks of Borneo, suggested by the dusky throng their arrival had attracted. As their eyes

where he established the pioneer overland mail route from San Antonio to San Diego.

Just when Ward had much association with Woods has not appeared. Most likely it was in San Francisco during 1852–54. It may even have been in 1861 about the time Ward was writing these reminiscences; for Woods, like Ward, was considered an authority on affairs in the infant Confederacy. Their friendship may have continued long after the publication of this memoir, for during the few years just before his death in 1880 Woods was manager of the large California ranch belonging to James R. Keene, at that time Sam Ward's closest friend.

had evidently failed to recognize me in the gloom, I spoke, and terminated a suspense quite as disagreeable to them as it might have proved unpleasant to me. It was, however, another of those occasions in which "a miss is as good as a mile," and we parted with a laugh, for the night.

After sharing my river-bath the next morning, my friend employed at the breakfast table a variety of arguments, some of them quite flattering, to persuade me that I had sufficiently prolonged my rustication, and should return to the more congenial and stirring scenes of active life. When he had left me it was his intention to push on to Mariposa that day, make some purchases of gold dust, examine the resources of the place, and, returning on the morrow, halt in Bear Valley, where I engaged to meet and present him to Major Killaly. The start of the four-horse team elicited a buzz of admiration and a discharge of *potoloks* from the savages, and having made my arrangements for a few day's absence I mounted Frémont and turned his head in the direction of Thorn Villa, where I was always glad of an excuse for taking a holiday. It must have been near noon when, in a little *canada* about three miles short of Quartzburg, I descried . . . . the stylish equipage of my guests at a stand-still in the bottom. Unable to imagine the cause of their perplexity, I hastened to them and found the wagon slightly stalled in a patch of mire from which the animals refused any effort to extricate it. They were California nags, unaccustomed to heavy draughts, and no persuasion or punishment could stimulate them to make the attempt. While awaiting the return of Colt, who had been dispatched to the village for a team of oxen, a couple of Mexican cavaliers came prancing down the road, one of whom I recognized as my competitor for the ounce won with the pistol. When informed of the cause of the embarrassments, they at once suggested that as the horses were natives, they needed only to be mounted to exert those powers of traction with which they were familiar in the "lassoing" of cattle. This happy idea was put into immediate execution by its advisers, who transferred their own saddles to the backs of the leaders, fastened one end of their *lassos* to the tongue of the wagon, took a turn with the other around the loggerheads of their saddles, and applying the spur, and simultaneously giving the shout of the *vaquero*, instantly brought into play the thews and sinews of the recusant steeds, who fairly flew up the hill with the liberated vehicle.

[This delay] compelled the tourists to expunge the inspection of Bear Valley from their *programme*, while affording me the unexpected pleasure of piloting them at once into the haven of Mrs. Thorn's hospitality, and of acting as a cicerone in the Washington Mine. . . . . Early in the afternoon, the gay turnout carried them off to Mariposa, and I returned to the river assured that I might expect them on the following evening.

I looked for them in vain, and ascribed their detention to "express" negotiations and arrangements, unexpectedly protracted. Early in the afternoon, however, the two *caballeros* made their appearance at our *pasada*, and baited their horses. The marksman challenged me to another trial of skill with the pistol, which resulted as before.[4] He lost, however, with great good temper, and I observed that he shot with a weapon a grade below the navy size. When ready for the road, they purchased a bottle of whiskey, a supply of hard bread, and a couple of rations of barley. To my surprise, instead of crossing the ferry, they rode leisurely down the river, and the last I saw of them was their silhouettes on the horizon as they disappeared over the bluffs.

[4] This was not Ward's last chance to prove he was a marksman; several years later he came back from a Paraguayan expedition with prizes won in shooting matches at Asunción.

In the forenoon of the following day, the express team made its appearance, having left Mariposa before sunrise after an instructive though otherwise improfitable day in the diggings, the party intending to bivouac at Heath & Emory's ferry that night. They remained only long enough to give their horses a bite, and take a cup of coffee in my sanctum, when Mr. Woods urged me to accompany him to San Francisco, "were it only for the 'lark' of a sixty miles drive behind so lively a team." I was unable, at the moment, to leave the *ranche*, but promised him, as he drove off, to follow him, if possible, later in the day, and overtake him at the Stanislaus so as to have the pleasure of entering Stockton in his triumphal car next morning.

Having made my arrangements, I selected my best charger—a cream color—and took the shortest cut to the Tuolumne. Shortly after striking the main road, about four miles beyond Snelling's, I noticed the track of a wagon, which had been abruptly turned off from the highway into the grass on the left towards the river. There were also marks of horses' hoofs in the turf, which grew into a hillock some twenty feet high on the right, its summit not more than thirty yards from the roadside. It struck me as a capital spot for an ambuscade, and I intuitively loosened the revolver in my belt, and kept "my eyes skinned" until I again reached level ground.

A new wayside inn had arisen between Dry Creek and Dickenson's since I had last passed up. It lacked an hour of sunset, and a smiling hostess in the doorway and a tethered cow hard by tempted me to try the fare of the establishment. This infidelity to my friend, the landlord of the Tuolumne, was recompensed by the unusual luxury of eggs and milk, for which I felt an eager longing. While at table, a well-grown lad came in with his rifle, complaining that the only game he had seen was a queer bird which appeared to run faster than it could fly, which he had shot, and thrown away, as it did not seem to be worth bringing home. Inferring from his description that the bird must have been that *rara avis*, a *paisano* or "chaparral cock," I offered the boy half a dollar to fetch it to me. While awaiting his return, a rider dashed up to the house and announced the startling news that a teamster had been shot upon the road that afternoon, robbed of six hundred dollars in gold dust, and his wagon driven into a clump of brushwood two miles from the road and there left with his corpse in it. Commending the people of the house to be on the alert, he spurred his horse towards Dickenson's Ferry, to give the "hue and cry" and ascertain whether any suspicious characters had crossed it that day. I instantly bethought me of the unusual wheel and horse prints I had noticed beneath the ambush where I had instinctively made ready for an attack, and argued that the crime could hardly have been perpetrated more than an hour previous to my passing. A murder in broad daylight sends an electric thrill through all who dwell far or near, and it was not without emotion that I remounted and continued my journey. I had scarcely ridden a hundred yards, when I heard the voice of the youngster who came running up with the *paisano* in his hands. I paid him his guerdon, and strung the bird, no longer so greatly coveted a prize, to my saddle bow. I quickened my pace so as to reach Dickenson's before dark, and was overtaken at the crossing by two horsemen, armed to the teeth, who were in pursuit of the murderers. From them I learned on the ferry boat that the victim was a son of one of the proprietors in our vicinity, a Snelling or a Montgomery—I forget which—a fine young man, who was on his way to purchase a load of goods at Stockton, and also that the deed had been done by not less than two assassins.[5]

[5] This murder was on April 28, 1852.

At Dickenson's I found quite a crowd discussing the murder, and proffering the usual variety of speculations as to its perpetrators. The theory which I had formed on the way shed a new light upon the catastrophe by fastening the suspicions of the assemblage upon the two *caballeros*, one of whom was so skillful a shot. I further surmised that they were in pursuit of higher game, viz., the bags of gold which they could not have failed to perceive in my friend Woods' wagon when they assisted in extricating it from the mire; that they had either missed him by an error of calculation, or had concluded that the party carried too many guns for them, and transferred their rapacity to the unfortunate teamster who must have come up not long after the express wagon had passed the fatal spot. If this supposition were true, the brigands must have made their escape by Waters' Ferry at the junction of the Merced with the San Joaquin, that being the only outlet into the lower country.

After feeding my horse, I pushed on to the Stanislaus, at first in the dark, which after an hour's ride was relieved by the light of the moon. To my surprise, my nerves, naturally excited by the recent casualty, became more sensitive as the obscurity was dispelled. Trees, bushes, and rocks assumed menacing proportions, or suggested ambuscades, which kept my hand on my pistol, until I finally drew it and carried it ready for use all the way to the ferry. A heavy growth of timber, a mile or more in depth, skirted the Stanislaus on that side, which I throde with a succession of mysterious apprehensions that only disappeared when the *halloo* from the house announced that my pistol shot had been heard by the ferryman, who lost no time in coming to my relief.

Although late at night when I reached the welcome verandah, I found the tap-room alive with guests and conjectures. . . . . My theory was received with favor—

no stranger had crossed there for several days, which I omitted to mention was also the case at Dickenson's. I found that my express friends had retired early and left orders for breakfast at daylight. . . . .

"I made a point" with my new companions by being up in season to share their breakfast and drive, notwithstanding the fatigue and agitations of the previous night. The day was charming, the road level, the team cheerful, and I felt more like a "gentleman" as we rolled along ten miles an hour, than I had in many a day. How I was induced to extend my jaunt to San Francisco, what befell me there and on my return, shall be reserved for another chapter. Meanwhile, I will anticipate any curiosity with which the reader may honor this narrative by adding here that the more persevering of the volunteer troop of friends who accompanied the relatives of the hapless young teamster in pursuit of his murderers at length overtook them, after a search of several days, more than a hundred miles beyond Pacheco's Pass, where, to save time and trouble, the verdict of an impartial jury was forestalled by the expeditious retribution of Judge Lynch. They had been tracked by my Indians, who were anxious to clear their own skirts of suspicions, to Waters' Ferry, which they crossed betimes on the afternoon of the murder and must have reached within four hours after its commission—a life-gallop of full forty miles. They met their fate with the usual composure of the Spanish race, and it may have been to gain time to smoke a cigarito when their doom became inevitable, that they confessed the deed which had been accomplished by a single bullet that found its way to the brain of the victim from the pistol of my rival marksman.

The serial memoir ended abruptly with this fourteenth installment, published in the issue of Porter's Spirit of the Times *for the week of April 23, 1861. The editor apologized to his subscribers, saying, "The illness of the author is our excuse." But Sam Ward was not ill. The year before, in London, he had been introduced by his friend Thackeray to William H. Russell, the famous war correspondent. When the* London Times *sent Russell to the United States in the spring of 1861, Sam Ward left New York and Washington to accompany him on a long trip behind the Confederate lines. In July the editor of* Porter's Spirit, *forgetting his earlier excuse, announced, "Our correspondent 'Midas, Jr.' has returned from his wanderings, and we anticipate a speedy renewal of the interesting series in our columns." But no more installments of the memoir appeared.*

Epilogue

JUST HOW SOON after May 1852 Sam Ward left the Merced is uncertain. But before the year ended he was in San Francisco, a directory listing his address as the Franklin Hotel. In the last months of 1852 and in early 1853 he sold some lots on Telegraph Hill. For a time in 1853 he lived in what he said was "a little shanty belonging to Mr. Price"; but by June he had moved in with Hall McAllister on Pike Street and afterward recalled, "I generally spent my days in the library." Captain, later General, Erasmus Keyes testified that from July 1, 1853, to January 1, 1854, he saw Sam Ward in San Francisco "almost daily, and was so charmed with the liveliness of his wit, his knowledge of languages, his skill in gastronomy" that he spent much of his time with Ward—in "feasting and vain discourses."

In August 1853 Rodman Price wrote to his California agent asking, "What is Ward doing? Is he making anything, or has he made any?" The agent's reply is not available, but judging by the slim evidence, Sam Ward was not making much in 1853; and he must not have "made any" in the next year, because his fortunes for the most part depended then on San Francisco real estate prices, which led the way to the bottom when the general depression began in the spring of 1854.

A review he wrote for the *Alta California* shows that he attended the opera in San Francisco on the last night of April 1854; this is the only positive evidence of his

173

whereabouts early in that year. But by autumn—just as he was leaving California—his affairs are a little clearer. A Frenchman, Count Raousset-Boulbon, led a filibustering expedition to Mexico in an attempt to take control of Sonora. He was defeated in July 1854 and imprisoned. Ward, who had known him in San Francisco, had been invited to accompany the expedition. He had refused, but when San Franciscans who also were friends of Boulbon asked Ward to go to Mexico to negotiate for the release of the Count and his men, he went. Because of the slowness of communications and the speed of the execution, Boulbon was dead before the writing of the letter which sent Sam to his aid; but Sam did go to Mexico City, and it is probable that he joined forces with the effective French diplomat, Dano, and contributed to the pressure which led Santa Anna to free Boulbon's followers. By December 5, 1854, Ward was again in the United States, at New Orleans.

From New Orleans he did not return to California but went to New York and then on a trip to Europe, beginning thirty years of activity which made him a celebrity here and abroad. Detailed accounts of that life are easily available, and this is not the place to describe it at length; but readers who have followed Sam Ward this far may want a brief summary of these later years.

He became a diplomatic agent in the employ of business firms and the State Department, making trips to South America to examine mines, to Paraguay as Secretary of Legation, to Nicaragua to look into filibustering and transportation across the Isthmus, to Europe on errands of all sorts, and to the western United States to deal with many people, among them Brigham Young.

In 1860 he became a lobbyist in Washington. At once he profited by his experience in the Gold Rush; for owners of California mineral lands were among his first clients, and the Senators from California were among the guests at his first small political dinners. He soon became "King of the Lobby," and reigned until the late 'seventies. Much that he did in Washington he was ashamed of, but he was proud of ending some harmful feuds and of acting effectively in preventing the impeachment of President Johnson. He gave the most elaborate dinners the capital had seen, and his development of this adjunct of lobbying made him so famous as a gourmet that Allan Nevins credits him with teaching America how to dine. During these years he was involved in the settlement of the *Alabama* claims, one of many issues which took him frequently across the Atlantic.

His youthful desire to be a writer still remained with him, finding many outlets. In addition to diaries, memoirs, articles, and innumerable letters, he wrote poems which appeared in the *Atlantic Monthly* and other periodicals, and were collected as *Lyrical Recreations*.

To his delight, many famous contemporaries were his friends, including Presidents Buchanan and Garfield, Thackeray, Agassiz, Seward, William Hurlbert of the *New York World*, Longfellow, Sumner, Lord Rosebery, and the Emperor of Brazil. Ward became so well known and well liked as a friend to foreigners visiting America that the London *Vanity Fair* said in 1880, "Every traveller to the United States whose lot has fallen in pleasant places is sure to have met with Samuel Ward, protector of the English and Uncle of the human race." In 1861, he had accompanied the war correspondent of the London *Times*, William H. Russell, on a tour in the Confederate States. After more than twenty years of such service as "Uncle of the human race," he completed that part of his career by guiding Oscar Wilde about New York and New England in 1882, becoming so much a part of the early weeks of that famous tour that he finally stopped traveling with

Wilde because, as he said, "I don't want to be eternally in the papers as his dry nurse."

As a reward for the services and the companionship which he gave to James R. Keene—a California financier who had invaded Wall Street—Sam Ward's third large fortune came to him in the late 'seventies. With it he enlarged his reputation as an authority on food, wines, and celebrities. When this fortune went the way of the others, in 1882, he became the guest of his friends Lord and Lady Rosebery in England, where he was a social lion of that London season.

In 1883 he went to Italy to visit members of his family, among them the novelist, F. Marion Crawford, who was his nephew and a great favorite with him. After several pleasant months there he fell ill. He died on May 19, 1884, at the age of seventy.

Bibliographical Note

AS STATED in the Preface, an interleaved copy of this book containing detailed references to sources of information is to be on deposit in the Stanford University Library, but a few of the general sources are listed here.

"Incidents on the 'River of Grace'" by "Midas, Jr." appeared in fourteen installments in *Porter's Spirit of the Times* between Volume IX, Number 22 (January 22, 1861), and Volume X, Number 9 (April 23, 1861). In republishing the serial here, approximately 12,000 words have been omitted.

Samuel Ward's life is given detailed treatment in Maud Howe Elliott's *Uncle Sam Ward and His Circle* (New York: Macmillian, 1938). Information about his life in California appears in San Francisco newspapers and directories; in legal documents in the Office of the Recorder of Mariposa County; in the printed documents of "The Supreme Court of the State of New York, City and County of New York: Rodman M. Price, Plaintiff, *against* Theodore Payne, Squire P. Dewey . . . . Defendants," *Cases in Court of Appeals, January, February, 1879*; in "Belt's Case," *Cases Decided in the Court of Claims at the December Term, 1879*, Washington, 1880, Volume XV; and in the manuscripts in the National Archives which concern that Court of Claims case.

Frank Maloy Anderson, *The Mystery of "A Public Man,"* University of Minnesota Press, published almost simultaneously with the publication of the present book and drawing the conclusion that Sam Ward's experiences formed the base for the famous "Diary of a Public Man" which has baffled historians for years, will be of value to readers interested in details of Ward's biography at the time he was writing for *Porter's Spirit* this serial memoir of the Gold Rush.

Mariposa County mining history appears in Newell D. Chamberlain's *The Call of Gold: True Tales on the Gold Road to Yosemite* (*Mariposa Gazette* Press, 1936); and in Charles G. Crampton's *The Opening of the Mariposa Mining Region, 1849–1859, With Particular Reference to the Mexican Land Grant of John Charles Frémont* (Ph.D. thesis, University of California, 1941). Rodman Paul's *California Gold* (Cambridge: Harvard University Press, 1947) is a useful study of California mining in general.

Specific information about the Indians who were at the Merced River reservation appears in *Senate Executive Document 4, Special Session, Thirty-third Congress*; and in the printed volume of evidence in "Belt's Case" mentioned above. A copy of the treaty signed by those Indians is in *Hearings Before the Committee on Indian Affairs, House of Representatives, Seventieth Congress, First Session, on H.R. 491.*

The newspapers containing the greatest number of items about Mariposa County during Samuel Ward's months there are the Stockton papers, consecutive files of which are available only in the Public Library of Stockton.

Acknowledgments

THE EDITOR is grateful to Maud Howe Elliott and The Macmillan Company for permission to quote from *Uncle Sam Ward and His Circle* and to reproduce von Vogelstein's portrait of Samuel Ward, which is the frontispiece of that book; to the Houghton Library for permission to quote from letters of Samuel Ward; to the Bancroft Library for permission to quote from the unpublished memoirs of Jessie Benton Frémont and to use the pictures reproduced on pages 48, 74, 135, 146, and 161; to the Huntington Library for permission to use the pictures reproduced on page 12 and facing pages 17 and 157; to the California State Library for permission to use the picture reproduced facing page 64; and to Edgar Eugene Robinson and the *California Historical Society Quarterly* for permission to quote from the "Day Journal" of Milton S. Latham, which Professor Robinson has edited.

For information and advice and for personal assistance, the editor is in debt to Frank Maloy Anderson, Newell D. Chamberlain, Bernard DeVoto, Lindley Eberstadt, Maud Howe Elliott, A. B. Guthrie, Jr., George G. Heye, William A. Jackson, Daniel Kidder, John L. O'Connor, Mark Schorer, Wallace Stegner, and Ruth Teiser.

For help in the final preparation of the text, the editor is grateful to Nancy W. Ignatius, Constance Nelson, and Virginia Proctor.

For their assistance, the editor is indebted to the staffs

of the Stanford University Press, the Houghton Library, the Bancroft Library, the Huntington Library, the Library of Congress, the Public Library of Stockton, the Office of the Recorder of Mariposa County, the California State Library, the Stanford University Library, and the National Archives.

Erwin Raisz and his assistants at Harvard University's Institute of Geographical Exploration were very co-operative in the preparation of the end-paper map.

Index

Rarey, J. S., 67, 69
Ricardo, David, 53
Ridout, Thomas Gibbs, 122
"River of Grace" (*see* Merced River)
Robinson, Edgar Eugene, 179
Rocky Mountains, 50, 153 n.
Rosebery, Archibald, Earl of, 175, 176
Rosebery, Lady, 176
Rothschild, Baron, 37, 43, 55 n.
Round Hill School, 3–4, 163 n.
Rue Quincampoix, 33
Russell, William H., 172, 175
Ruxton, George Frederick, 50, 75–76, 154

Sabine (frigate), 116 n.
Sacate, 68–74, 78–84, 87–92, 94, 141
Sacramento, 20, 137
San Antonio, 54, 165 n.
San Diego, 165 n.
San Francisco, 3, 7, 11, 13, 14, 15–16, 19, 26 n., 27 n., 29 n., 31, 34, 42, 45–46, 47, 50–51, 57 n., 59 n., 60 n., 61, 66, 70, 72–74, 79, 81, 84, 90, 95, 103, 105–6, 107 n., 125, 126 n., 130, 137, 145, 147, 149, 150 n., 164 n., 168, 171, 173–74, 177
San Joaquin County, 54 n.
San Joaquin Republican, 41 n., 54 n.
San Joaquin River, 26 n., 27, 60 n., 84, 91, 156, 170
San Joaquin Valley, 54 n., 108 n.
San Jose, 84, 85, 90, 91
Sand, George, 9

Santa Anna, Antonio López de, 77, 78 n., 174
Sarg (Frankfort hotel keeper), 134
Savage, James, 57 n., 59–63, 64, 92, 114
Say, Jean Baptiste, 53
Schorer, Mark, 179
Scott, Sir Walter, 35, 147 n.
Seward, William Henry, 175
Shaw (British Guardsman), 119
Sibley, A. H., 34 n., 147–52
Sierra Nevada, 26 n., 27, 148
Sim, William, 150–52
Sirey & Clark's Ferry, 20–21
Slidell, John, 100
Smith, Adam, 53
Smith, P. T., 119–23, 125, 127, 128, 130
Snelling, Mr., 169
Snelling's Ranche, 21–22, 168
Société de Géographie, 5
Socrates, 37
Soda Springs, Idaho, 50
Sonora, Calif., 41 n.
Sonora, Mexico, 27 n., 174
Sophie (steamer), 20, 46, 70, 71–72, 75, 80–81, 105
Sorbonne, 5
South America, 14, 174
Southern Mines, 10, 16, 20 n., 28 n., 41, 51–52, 61 n., 113 n., 147 n., 162
Soyer, Alexis, 25
Staël, Madame de, 148
Stakes, A. G., Judge, 54
Stanford University Library, vi, 177, 180
Stanislaus River, 20, 21 n., 22, 76, 78, 104, 122, 168, 170
Stegner, Wallace, 179

INDEX

Ward, Henry (Sam Ward's
  brother), 9
Ward, John (Sam Ward's uncle),
  10, 15
Ward, John Randolph (Sam
  Ward's son), 10
Ward, Julia Rush (Sam Ward's
  mother), 4
Ward, Margaret (Sam Ward's
  daughter), 10
Ward, Marion (Sam Ward's
  brother), 9, 10
Ward, Medora Grymes (Sam
  Ward's second wife), 9, 10
Ward, Samuel (Sam Ward's fath-
  er), 4, 6, 9, 10
Ward, Samuel (son of Sam Ward),
  10
Ward & Price, 11, 14–15
Washington, D.C., 54 n., 55 n.,
  100, 105, 111, 174–75
Washington Mine, 28–29, 30–31,
  45, 89, 94–98, 100–103, 105–
  7, 124, 147 n., 149, 167

Waters' Ferry, 170, 171
Weber, Charles M., 20
Whisman, J. W., 136 n.
White, Billy, 164
Wilde, Oscar, 175–76
Williams, William Sherley ("Old
  Bill"), 154–55
Wilson (ferryman), 109, 112,
  121
Wind River Range, 50, 154
Wisconsin, 96
Woodruff, E., 31 n.
Woods, Mr. Isaiah C., 164–67,
  168, 170, 171
Wozencraft, Oliver M., 56 n.
Wright, George W., 40 n.

Yancey, William Lowndes, 100
Young, Brigham, 174
Young, John Radford, 4
Young, Thoroughgood W. T.,
  127 n.

Zacatecas, Mexico, 35, 42

189